Living in the Father's Embrace

Experiencing the Love at the
Heart of the Trinity

Living in the Father's Embrace

Experiencing the Love at the
Heart of the Trinity

George T. Montague, SM

theWORD
among us®
press

Published by The Word Among Us Press
7115 Guilford Drive
Frederick, Maryland 21704

18 17 16 15 14   1 2 3 4 5

ISBN: 978-1-59325-253-3
eISBN: 978-1-59325-457-5

Cover design by John Hamilton Designs
Cover art: *The Return of the Prodigal Son*
Bartolome Esteban Murillo (1618–1682)
Location: National Gallery of Art, Washington, D.C.
Photo Credit: Album/Art Resource, NY

Made and printed in the United States of America

Library of Congress Control Number: 2014935220

Contents

Introduction: Invitation / 7

1. The Embrace / 11

2. Blocks / 19

3. Eavesdropping on Jesus / 25

4. Healing the Father Wound, Part I / 31

5. Healing the Father Wound, Part II / 37

6. Wounds of Spouses and Peers / 43

7. Pure Eyes, Pure Heart / 49

8. Asleep in the Storm / 55

9. Papa, You're Too Big! / 59

10. The Name, the Kingdom, the Will / 65

11. Bread for His Children / 71

12. Father's Breast, Mother's Breast / 77

13. When the Father Takes Away / 83

14. Risk and Rescue / 91

15. Transformer / 97

16. Other Fathers / 103

17. Jesus, Icon of the Father / 111

18. Brothers and Sisters / 115

19. The Father Embraces His Family / 121

20. Jesus Prays to His Father for Us / 127

About the Author / 134

Introduction

Invitation

When the image of your father comes to your mind, what happens to your heart? Does it grow warm? Or is it chilled? If your father is absent, do you long to see him, or are you glad he is away? Perhaps your reaction is neither warm nor cold but tepid—there are some things you like about your father and some things you don't.

I have often reflected on how I felt about my own father, and I will share that with you in this book. But as a priest, I have been fascinated by the different kinds of fathers I have encountered in the hearts of their children. Not the fathers themselves, but as they are housed in their children's hearts. For that is the place where mighty things happen, for good or ill. The father image is often the lens through which we view the world and the judgment we make on others. And most often, at least for a long while, we are unaware of the lens.

But it is there. If our father was peaceful in his approach to problems or problem people, we will tend to be the same. If he was violent, we may tend to be violent. And what about our image of *God*? Both from my own experience and that of scores of others, I can say that the image we have of our father goes a long way in telling us who God is, especially when we learn to call him "Father." If our father image has been joyful, meeting

God the Father will normally be joyful. But if our father image has been painful, the encounter with God will likely be hobbled with distrust. In any case, our relationship with our earthly father has a tremendous effect on our image of God.

I have wanted to write this book because my many years of pastoral experience have convinced me that most people need healing of the "father wound." Fathers are meant to give us security as we are growing up, an example of how to live in a challenging world, and love that is strong and persevering. But if God wanted us to have perfect parents, he would have made them that way. So we have to accept the father we've been given. Yet our hearts long for the perfect father, and as we grow up, we find that expectation frustrated, and sometimes even dashed to the ground.

But healing is possible. God does not want us to be slaves of our origins or our past. Our God is a God of exodus, a God of liberation, a God constantly inviting us to leave the old and embrace the new. He has a promised land awaiting us even in this life. And one of the names of that promise is *Abba*.

But this book is about more than healing the father wound. Whether we were close to our earthly father or emotionally distant, to meet our heavenly Father is to experience our father-dream fulfilled beyond our wildest expectations. Even the best human fathers are finite. God is infinitely Father.

Maybe we say that we have met Jesus, and that is enough. But is it? Jesus tells us, "No one knows the Son except the Father, and no one knows the Father except the Son *and anyone to whom the Son wishes to reveal him*" (Matthew 11:27, emphasis mine). That means that only the Father really knows Jesus, and if we really want to know Jesus, we had better ask the Father to show us who Jesus really is. And by the same token, to know the Father as Jesus knows him—and that is the only way—Jesus must give us the gift of his own experience of the Father.

That is what this book is about: meeting the Father. If it helps you to do that, then even if you were the only reader, that is reward beyond measure.

Father George

Jesus, lay your hands upon my head at this moment and send me the Holy Spirit to teach me to know the Father as you know him, to call him "Abba." As I read, may your Spirit breathe upon my heart and enlighten my mind to this mystery of Trinitarian LOVE.

Chapter 1

The Embrace

Uniformed and gaunt, Robert Stirm stepped from the plane onto the first land he could call home in six years. A prisoner of war in North Vietnam, the now-liberated Air Force lieutenant colonel looked up to see his family racing toward him. His wife, two sons, and two daughters were more than racing—flying, rather, because a photographer caught the pack of five with only two feet on the ground. In the lead was his sixteen-year-old daughter, her arms thrown wide like wings. The miniskirted lass with platform shoes aloft, eyes saucer-sized, would in the next second collide with her dad in a hug, releasing a longing pent up for six years. And their first shared breath would probably not even be a word, but love exploding in a shout of wordless joy. The joy would then ripple to the rest of the family.

That moment in 1973 was only a blip in the life of one family's history. But imagine what it is like for God the Father to embrace his Son in a mutual ecstasy, which, though unending, never loses the freshness of a first encounter. And what would we expect? The same kind of explosion that happened between the airman father and his daughter, except that in God, we call this explosion the Holy Spirit.

We would never have known that about God—about Father, Son, and Holy Spirit—if all we had were our human reason.

Others have reasoned or come to believe that there is only one God. And billions of people have worshipped the Creator. After all, it is pretty difficult to look at the stars, even more so today with the help of the Hubble telescope, and not let your jaw drop. And if you ask why we *are*, why we exist at all, the answer is that we don't *have* to. We didn't have anything to do with our coming into the world. We are gift, sheer gift. And gift means there is a Giver. So awe leading to reverence, and even to worship of the Creator, is within the powers of the human mind—though we can suspect that somehow God's grace works with the goodwill of those who don't know that there is more.

But to know the inner mystery of God? To break the sight and sound barrier between the finite and the infinite? Only if God, not us, would choose to do so.

He did. The Author of those light-year expanses peopled by billions of stars and still undiscovered galaxies not only made us. He chose to befriend us, to tell us not just *that* he is, but *who*. And if he chooses to tell us who he is, it is because he wishes to initiate a personal relationship with us.

How did he do that? We might expect that he would have choosen some kind of celestial sign, or a design cut out in a field of wheat, or the landing of a spacecraft—something dramatic that would grab our attention and let us glimpse flashes of the mystery. But no, he slipped in, first as a tiny cell in a mother's womb, then birthed on straw, the food of a service animal. He was welcomed only by his mother, her husband, Joseph, and night-watching shepherds. The bridge between the divine and the human, the infinite and the finite, was built of human flesh, and the infinite reach of that bridge was hidden in a baby's cry.

Unnoticed for decades, he grew up as a normal child—*perfectly* normal, as no sin-lashed man could be—and if there was anything surprising about him, it was just how shockingly human he was. A good carpenter, yes, and gifted with wit and wisdom amid his peers, until he was about the age of thirty, when, like others of his day, he took off for the Jordan River to be baptized by a fire-and-brimstone preacher named John the Baptist. Otherwise, no one thought of him as especially qualified to reveal the face of God—even more so because he queued up with the rest of the penitents and waited his turn. A nice fellow, but a sinner like the rest, coming to confess his sins. So it seemed. No one at the time realized whose sins he was carrying—and burying.

But that changed when he came out of the water. Water quenches fire, but as with Elijah confronting the false prophets on Mount Carmel, this water only hastened fire. Coming out of the water, Jesus of Nazareth was on fire, consumed by the Holy Spirit and commissioned by the voice that revealed him as the Son of God. It was Jesus himself who first experienced it, for Mark says Jesus saw the heavens being torn open and the Spirit coming upon him like a dove. He saw the dove and heard the voice: "You are my beloved Son; with you I am well pleased" (Mark 1:11).

The Father Revealed through the Son

Who, then, is this "normal" man? He is one who stands in a unique relationship with God. He is God's Son in a way that no one else could ever be. He is not adopted; he is begotten. As we know from the tradition and the teaching of the Church, this baptismal event in time reveals a relationship prior to and outside of time: the eternal relationship of Father and Son. And in revealing Jesus as his Son, God also reveals himself: he is Father. There is, then, at the baptism, a simultaneous interpersonal revelation: God the Father, God the Son.

This is no small matter. Not everyone in the world knows of this revelation, and still fewer accept it. There are atheists who have convinced themselves that there is no God, either misled by specious reasoning or because they live as if there is no God. Then there are those who believe in some kind of force in nature, which they call God, or who believe that everything is God (animists, pantheists). Then there are those who believe in many gods, gods who dispute their powers with each other. Finally, there are the monotheists, those who belong to one of the three great world religions: Islam, Judaism, and Christianity. Islam has a powerful sense of God as Creator, but it refuses to call God Father (that would bring God too close, especially if he has a Son). Judaism also hails God as Creator, and in addition, he is a God who has sealed a covenant with his people Israel. The chosen people know him by many titles—Lord, King, Shepherd, Rock, Fortress, and yes, Father—but it is always the formal title, appearing roughly a dozen times in the Old Testament.

But Christians contemplating Jesus' baptism see an icon of the inner life of God. And they see Father, whom Jesus will call *"Abba,"* the intimate "Daddy." Yes, that intimate. Prostrate in agony, Jesus cries out, *"Abba,* Father, all things are possible to you. Take this cup away from me, but not what I will but what you will" (Mark 14:36).

That *"Abba"* Jesus cried to God in the garden came from an adult voice and an adult heart. But where, in Jesus' development from childhood (he grew in "wisdom and age and favor," Luke 2:52), did he first say *"Abba"*? It was not in the synagogue, where he first heard all those other biblical titles. Beautiful as they were to him, he had an experience of human fatherhood that went far beyond them. It was in his home that this sacred child first said *"Abba,"* for that is what he called Joseph.

There is a cornucopia of consequences here for the vocation of fatherhood, which we shall explore later. But for the time being, let us return to our contemplation of that eternal relationship of Jesus with the *Abba* "who art in heaven" (cf. Matthew 6:9).

What must that infinitely intimate relationship that Jesus has with the Father be like! What must it be for Jesus to be constantly face-to-face with God as his only begotten Son, begotten yet equal because he is the very image of the Father! The human words Jesus uses in telling us to pray "Our Father" are but a faint trace of the reality that Jesus himself experiences. And we would have no access to that interpersonal mystery if it were not for the other agent in the baptism icon, the Holy Spirit.

Communion and Mission

At the grotto of Our Lady of Lourdes, its sprawling campus shaded by San Antonio live oaks, there appeared for several weeks a pair of white doves that took turns, one perching on the head of Mary while the other nestled at her feet. Not native to Texas, they seemed to have a natural affection for her. The image invited others to think of the Holy Spirit, who overshadowed this Lady to work the miracle of the Incarnation and then stayed with her in an eternal covenant. White doves appeared at his window when Pope John Paul II delivered one of his last Angelus messages. And in many cultures, especially in the Hispanic culture, the dove is the messenger of love. So it was already in the Old Testament's romantic Song of Songs, in which the dove appears six times. So in the baptism of Jesus, the dove is the visible symbol of the Father's love, giving visual confirmation of his audible voice declaring Jesus his beloved.

But the Father is also the beloved of Jesus, and just as in marriage the gift of rings symbolizes the unending bond of love between man and wife, so the dove reveals the eternal bond of love between Father and Son. From elsewhere in the New Testament and the Tradition of the Church, we know that the Holy Spirit is actually a Person equal in majesty to the Father and the Son, from whom the Spirit proceeds. Thus, the drama in the Jordan reveals in time the eternal communion of love in the Trinity.

But the baptism reveals more than something of the inner life of God. The baptism is the consecration of Jesus in his humanity for his mission to his people and to the world. Passing first through testing in the desert, he will launch his public life with preaching and healing and ultimately offering himself in sacrifice for the sins he drowned in the Jordan. As he often says in the Gospels, he is *sent*. "The Spirit of the Lord is upon me, / because he has anointed me to bring glad tidings to the poor. / He has sent me to proclaim liberty to captives / and recovery of sight to the blind, to let the oppressed go free, / and to proclaim a year acceptable to the Lord" (Luke 4:18-19). Unlike the world's gurus and Israel's rabbis, Jesus will not only teach but pass through the transforming fire of his passion to the glory of the resurrection and call all people to share in that mystery. How? By their own baptism, they share in his. Communion in the mystery of Jesus' death and resurrection will lead to their own experience of the Trinitarian life of God.

And that means both communion and mission. And here we see another symbolic function of the dove. For there is another place in the Bible where the dove plays a revealing role. Noah, afloat with a remnant of the world destroyed by the flood, sees the waters beginning to subside. He sends out a raven to see if any dry land has appeared, only to lament its return with an empty beak. Finally, Noah sends out a dove that returns with an olive branch. The dove and the branch announce a new creation. God is starting to make the world anew (Genesis 8:6-12).

That is what happened when Jesus was baptized. As Jesus stood over the waters, the dove told the world that God was beginning an extreme makeover, a new, more beautiful world. Jesus called it "the kingdom of God." And that is what happens whenever a Christian is baptized. Be he or she only an infant, God is beginning to recreate the world starting with that person. Such is the awesome dignity and responsibility God gives us by our baptism. Noah celebrated the new beginning with a sacrifice. Jesus' sacrifice makes the new creation possible. The baptized Christian applies the fruits of that sacrifice to his particular role in time and history.

Jesus lives in the Father's embrace in eternity and in time. And from their mutual love flows the Holy Spirit, the river of living water that flows from the throne of God and the Lamb (Revelation 22:1). By faith and baptism, we are caught up in their mutual embrace, like a child kissed simultaneously on either cheek by father and mother.

How do we experience and then live in that awesome divine embrace? That's what the rest of this book is about.

....

Father, I am overwhelmed by your gift—first of all, for my very life. I did nothing to merit my coming into existence. I am gift, your gift. But I would never have known you in your intimate life had you not chosen to share that secret with me. In sending your son Jesus and the Holy Spirit, you have given me a share in your own interpersonal love. I can love you with the heart of your Son and love him with your love. And that mysterious bond of mutual love, the Holy Spirit, has drawn me into that embrace. My head is already spinning and my heart is dancing. May I grow in understanding the gift and live in anticipation of the day when I will see you face-to-face. Amen.

FOR REFLECTION

1. What is or was your relationship with your father? Good? Bad? Mixed?

2. How do you think your relationship with your father affects or affected your image of God?

3. What difference does it make that you know God, not as a force, not merely as Creator, but as a Father who wants a loving relationship with you?

CHAPTER 2

Blocks

hat is it like to live without the Father's embrace? Instead of Eden, it is desert. We may not realize it at first, just as the prodigal son thought his share of the father's gold would equip him to make an Eden of his own (Luke 15:11-32). So off he went, not aware of what he was leaving but glad to be free of it. The father did not bar the door against his son's folly, for what would it be worth to have a captive and a slave living in his home instead of a son bound only by love? Would the fleeing son die in his folly, or would the reality of a fatherless life, drained even of his father's gold, awaken him? For the father, the question goes unanswered; he lives in a wasteland of the unknown. And so, unknowingly, does the son live in a wasteland of his own.

It is a crossroads that all of us face at one time or another in our lives. Jesus compared the choice between two roads, one wide and easy, the other narrow and steep: the road of irresponsible pleasure that ends in death, or Jesus' road of sacrificial love that brings delight in the gift of self and ends in the Father's eternal embrace (Matthew 7:13-14). But as prodigals still bent on building our own kingdom, we often need to taste first the famine to which our choices have led us. If we hit bottom and are so famished that pig food would be a delicacy, that, strangely, is grace. It is the hidden voice of the Father telling us that our pangs are really nothing more than our own choices screaming to us that they are not God and telling us to go back before it is too late.

Yearning for the ample food even the hired help enjoys in his father's house, the son gets up, aware that his hunger is for more than food. He longs for his father's embrace, which he no longer deserves. "Father, I have sinned against heaven and against you. I no longer deserve to be called your son; treat me as you would treat one of your hired workers" (Luke 15:18-19). With that, he gets up and takes the long journey home.

This story tells us that we cannot presume to gain the Father's embrace if our own choices have made it impossible. We call that block attachment to sin. If our lifestyle blocks the very happiness the Father wants for us, if we cling to what we know is wrong, blind to the truth that confronts us at every turn, then we need, like the prodigal, to come to our senses. We need to repent and confess that we are unworthy of even the slightest nod of the Father's mercy. Undeserving though we are, we need to go home. God's providence has shown us that there is nowhere else to go.

The good news is that there is nowhere else we would want to go. Exhausted and stumbling and fearing the Father's wrath, we no sooner catch sight of home than we see the Father. We would run to him had we the strength—but look, he is running to us, his right arm extended to embrace us, his left hand holding up the skirt of his robe, heedless of the comic necessity his running demands. Tears cut furrows in our cheeks as we fall to our knees and begin to recite the confession we have rehearsed. The Father does not let us finish but lifts us up and clasps us to his breast. He, too, has tears—our tears of sorrow met by his of joy.

An Embrace of Mercy

So it is that the Father's embrace of us is inescapably and always an embrace of mercy. Unmerited mercy, for we are sinners, but mercy compelled by God's love that had never left us, even when we had left him. The Father not only welcomes; he restores—with robe, ring, and sandals. Not only is the bond between father and son restored, but the family bond as well. The Father orders a celebration for family and community. We have here all the elements of the Sacraments of Reconciliation and the Eucharist: confession and forgiveness and the festive meal celebrating redemption of the lost or, as the Father will say, a resurrection: "[He] was dead and has come to life again" (Luke 15:32).

But in the music that fires the dancing, there is a minor chord. As the father looks over the crowd, he notices one missing: the elder son. Where is he, and why doesn't he join the party? As the father had run to the younger son, he seeks out the elder, only to find him angry and bitter. "I have slaved for you all these years, and this son of yours [not "my brother"] comes back after blowing his inheritance on prostitutes, and you throw a barbecue for him." The father would embrace him but realizes the son is not ready and would reject the embrace.

The elder son is caught in the snare of his own unforgiveness. He cannot share his father's joy because he cannot share his father's forgiveness. Ironically, he is more lost than his brother, because he is lost and does not know it.

If the younger son tells the story of our wasted pursuit of reckless pleasure, the elder tells the story of our unwillingness to forgive. If the younger son was lost in a foreign land, the elder is locked in a prison. It is a maximum-security prison of his own making, the prison of the heart. He thinks he has locked his brother (and yes, even his father) in that prison, unaware that it is he who is the prisoner. As the younger brother is ourselves, so too is the elder. If we cannot feel the Father's embrace as long as we cling to the foreign land of sin, neither can we if we lock our hearts through anger, hatred, bitterness, or unforgiveness. We must go home. We must release our brother and join the party. And we must embrace our brother so that the Father can embrace us. That's all he is waiting for.

Does the son enter? The story doesn't say, because at this point the elder son is you and I, and we will decide how the story ends.

....

Father, I long for your embrace. But I am far away, victim of my own folly and of my broken bond with you. I want to go home. It was so much better there. Let me feel your forgiveness when you embrace me. And may my elder brother forgive me as you have, for I must ask his forgiveness too. May we both enjoy the feast you have prepared. Amen.

FOR REFLECTION

1. Do you have children or a friend or acquaintance that is living the lifestyle of the prodigal son? What does that person's state lead you to do?

2. Have you ever found yourself in the prodigal's shoes? In the shoes of the elder son?

3. Have you ever struggled with forgiveness? What helped you to overcome your bitterness?

CHAPTER 3

Eavesdropping
on Jesus

In Canada, a woman named Laura Secord is honored as a heroine. She even has a candy named after her. Her achievement? Eavesdropping. As the story goes, she overheard American officers planning their attack on the English in the War of 1812, then walked a cow to the English side with information that enabled them to win the Battle of Beaver Dams. There are other versions of the story, but this one is the most popular.

The disciples of Jesus eavesdropped on his prayer, or so St. Luke lets us surmise: "He was praying in a certain place, and when he had finished, one of his disciples said to him, 'Lord, teach us to pray, just as John taught his disciples'" (Luke 11:1). This was a strange request, because every Jew knew how to pray, having learned both at home and in the synagogue. But there was something different about Jesus' prayer, and they wanted the key to the mystery. First of all, it was his habit to withdraw not only from the crowds but even from his own disciples when he wanted to pray (Mark 1:35-37; Luke 22:41; John 6:15). But what was most surprising is that he addressed God as *"Abba"* (Mark 14:36). That was the intimate form, never used in the Bible for the Lord. The disciples were not used to that degree of intimacy with God. But for Jesus, it seemed so natural that the disciples judged it to be authentic, though they wouldn't have dared to use that word themselves.

Jesus must have understood their discomfort in telling them that *they* should address God that way, so at the end of the little instruction on prayer, he tells them, "Ask and you will receive. . . . What *father* among you would hand his son a snake when he asks for a fish? Or hand him a scorpion when he asks for an egg? If you then, who are wicked, know how to give good gifts to your children, how much more will the *Father* in heaven give the *holy Spirit* to those who ask him?" (Luke 11:9, 11-13; emphasis mine). In reporting these words of Jesus, St. Luke is anticipating the gift of the Holy Spirit at Pentecost. The Spirit will bridge the gap between the disciples' sense of unworthiness before the infinite God and the intimacy with the Father that will enable them to cry "*Abba*" with the heart and the holiness of Jesus. If their unworthiness makes them feel like the shoe-shed Moses before the burning bush, daring not to approach so great a fire, the Holy Spirit sweeps them into the fire itself, the fire that is God's own inter-Trinitarian love. And there they can taste Jesus' own love of the Father when they say "*Abba.*"

That is something totally beyond our human capacity. It is grace, pure grace; it is gift, pure gift. St. Paul says that the Holy Spirit bears united witness with our spirit that we are the children of God (Romans 8:16), and the Spirit enables us to cry, "*Abba, Father!*" (Galatians 4:6). At the moment that Jesus taught his disciples the Lord's Prayer, they probably did not understand, but they would when the Holy Spirit had come upon them. So it is with us. As with the disciples, we won't know what the words of the Lord's Prayer—and most especially the word "*Abba*"—mean without the Holy Spirit.

Thirsting for the Holy Spirit

But Jesus assures us that we can have that Holy Spirit for the asking. Our asking cannot, however, be routine. It must be passionate and persevering. That is the meaning of Jesus' story just before he tells us to ask (Luke 11:5-8). A midnight visitor arrives, and the family provider has no bread to set before him. So the host has to go next door and bang repeatedly on the neighbor's door, even after refusals, until finally the neighbor gets up and hands him an armful of loaves. God wants us to nag and keep nagging, because the process deepens our desire and our capacity to receive and appreciate the gift once given.

So how badly do we want the Holy Spirit? How badly do we thirst for him? Are we like the cowboy who sings, "All day I've faced the barren waste without a taste of water, cool water"? If you don't remember the song, think of the time when you were so thirsty that you thought of nothing else but water. That's the thirst we should have for the Holy Spirit. It means dropping all other priorities until we reach the well of living water.

And what happens when we get there? I cannot tell you because you have to experience it for yourself. All I can say is that you are experiencing a creature's share in Jesus' experience of the Father. You have been granted entry into the unimaginable depths of the Godhead, the eternal gaze of the Son upon the Father on whose breast he rests (John 1:18). St. Paul says as much when he writes that "eye has not seen, ear has not heard, nor has it ever entered the mind of man, what God has prepared for those who love him," yet this is what "God has revealed to us through the Spirit. For the Spirit searches out everything, even the depths of God"

(1 Corinthians 2:9, 10; my translation). The Holy Spirit is thus the searchlight, revealing things about God that we would never dream of. He is like the lights and camera, sunk to the depths of the Atlantic and revealing the Titanic, or a guide throwing a powerful flashlight on a cavern wall and showing us an awesome, eons-old water-crafted pillar. But the Father is no Titanic, nor is he an awesome pillar. He is . . . no words will do. Let the word-less Word carry you from here.

That is why Paul describes the work of the Holy Spirit in our prayer as groaning beyond words. In his Letter to the Romans, he applies it not only to our prayer to God but to our prayer for everything else, a prayer that joins us to the Holy Spirit's intercession for the world and for the completion of God's plan for all creation. "The Spirit comes to the aid of our weakness; for we do not know how to pray as we ought, but the Spirit himself intercedes with inexpressible groaning" (8:26, my translation). It is a groaning that echoes and leads the groaning of all creation for cosmic redemption, the bringing of all creation into the kingdom of God (8:23), when Christ will hand over the kingdom he has won to the Father (1 Corinthians 15:24).

The bosom of the Father is thus the goal of all our prayer, be it contemplation or intercession. When led by the Holy Spirit, we pray as God wants us to pray, and he understands what the Spirit is saying when we do not (Romans 8:27). When the Holy Spirit takes over our prayer, we find ourselves lifted beyond ourselves to the mystery that even the holiest thoughts cannot grasp. Such was the function of the gift of tongues in the prayer of the early Church, and the prayer gift that many experience today.

Words, though inadequate, are not inappropriate. In fact, they are necessary to give starlight when, in the night of this world, we don't have heaven's sun. They are truths about God such as we find in the Creed and the *Catechism*. It is important to remember, however, that behind and through all the words is a personal God who longs to be one with us in love, Trinitarian love, the interpersonal love of Father and Son to which we are given access through the Holy Spirit.

This life in the Spirit is not a once-done event. It is meant to grow in us. So we can never say that we have completely experienced all that the Spirit has to give. We can expect new departures from time to time. Such a departure happened in my own life on Christmas Eve 1970 when friends prayed over me for a release of the Holy Spirit. It was certainly not the first time I had received the Holy Spirit. Baptized, confirmed, recipient of Holy Communion for years, a professed religious and ordained priest, I had certainly been lavishly visited by the Holy Spirit. But I believe the Holy Spirit is like a time-release capsule, the full effect of which happens on a timetable not completed by the first swallow. Or maybe like the century plant, the Spanish *agave* that can sit for years in your front yard and then one day, unannounced, begin to shoot up to a height of twenty feet and display a crown of gold.

Different people have different experiences when touched anew by the Holy Spirit. Some experience a new closeness to Jesus. Some find that Scripture comes alive for them. Some receive one of the charismatic gifts like tongues, prophecy, or healing. For me, the primary gift of this renewal in the Spirit was meeting God the Father. To experience the Father's embrace at this new degree of intimacy was overwhelming. And that leads to the next chapter.

....

Jesus, lay your hand upon me and say, "Receive the Holy Spirit." I seek not only purification but infilling. Let me experience that inner artesian well of which you spoke to the Samaritan woman, that living water (John 4:10). You promised it to those who simply asked. Because you promised, I already thank you for hearing my prayer. Amen.

FOR REFLECTION

1. Why do we need the Holy Spirit to have the experience of God as *Abba*?

2. What do we need to do to prepare ourselves for a new outpouring of the Holy Spirit?

3. How do our words to and about God both reveal and conceal him?

CHAPTER 4

Healing the Father Wound, Part I

I am going to speak here about the father wound because for me this was, and for many others still is, the biggest block to experiencing intimacy with the Father, *Abba*. For many others it is the mother wound that is deepest. Some have experienced both the father and the mother wound. I once presided at a Mass for children who had been taken away from both parents because of abuse. At the prayers of the faithful, one of the boys prayed for his dog. Touched by that, I shared it with one of the supervisors at the orphanage. He replied, "Yes, that's probably because his dog is the only one who ever showed him love." Something inside me screamed at this tragedy.

Compared to this little boy's horrible launch into life, my experience was like the annoyance of a gnat. It made me grateful for the father and mother I had. Yet as a boy, I lacked that appreciation of my father because of the woundedness I felt. And I pray that my father will forgive me for sharing his faults in a public way. I do so only so that my experience—and his—will help others.

Papa was a big man, big in many ways. He stood six feet tall without his boots and Stetson hat, and it took a size fifty-five belt to circle his two hundred and eighty pounds. No wonder his grandchildren would call him "Big Daddy." In contrast to his slender son, Frank Junior, everyone knew him as "Big Frank." He was wonderfully good in many ways—in the gifts that he gave me and in the time that he spent with me hunting or fishing or taking me with him to the small-town bank, of which he was president. One scene has always reminded me of how really big he was.

For some reason, my mother was not at home, leaving my Aunt Margaret as her replacement to cook supper. We stood at the table to say grace, Papa at the head of the table and Aunt Margaret opposite me. After grace, it occurred to me to act like the gentleman I wanted to grow up to be, so I moved around to pull out the chair for Aunt Margaret. But in the split second between pulling it out and pushing it back, a little devil sat on my left shoulder and whispered, "What would happen if you wouldn't push the chair back?" My guardian angel commandeered my right shoulder, but not in time to win. Aunt Margaret went down, not quite hitting the floor because I caught her in time. But like a rattler striking, a sting hit my left cheek—Papa's reflexive slap. Aunt Margaret, whose regard for me was unconditionally positive, came quickly to my defense: "But he was only trying to be helpful." Papa grunted, about the only sound for the rest of the meal. I toyed with my food, happy when done to escape to my bed upstairs, only to be choked there by guilt and confusion.

But the drama was not over. I heard the sound of Papa's boots, announcing all two hundred and eighty pounds of him coming up the stairs. I could count each step, and yes, he reached the one that creaked; and on he came until his huge frame filled the doorway, and it was time for me to say the Act of Contrition. But suddenly his huge frame collapsed to his knees at my bedside, and he said, "George, I'm sorry I struck you. I shouldn't have done that. Please forgive me." Stunned, all I could say was "That's all right." Then Papa kissed me on the forehead and wished me goodnight.

As I said, Papa was a big man. [Footnote: By a series of rare circumstances, in my elder years I was given the opportunity to share that story on National Public Radio.]

And yet, despite all that, I had a fear of my father. I was pigeon-toed from birth, and this seemed to anger my father, who would shout at me, "George, walk straight!" And there were a few times that this embarrassing correction happened in public. His anger could flare in an instant, and while that slap on my face was the only flash of physical violence I ever saw in my home, still Papa was a volcano that could explode, and we were careful to tiptoe around it. As a result, my transfer of my father image to God was quite unlike that of Jesus in relation to Joseph. God, to my child's mind, was simply Papa to the nth degree—meaning, tiptoe around God.

Healing through Forgiveness

That father wound crippled me for a long time by leading me to transfer my father image to other authorities. But that, too, was part of my healing as I encountered other father figures in my religious life who freed me from the volcano myth. And in the process, God himself has freed me from seeing him as a volcano. God the Father has taught me that he is a God of liberation, a God of exodus. He does not want us to live in bondage to the Pharaohs of our memories. Years later in a midnight prayer—my Gethsemane—I was able to confront my deceased father, forgive him, and allow him to forgive me. Yes, forgive *me* for the things I had done to hurt *him*, for full reconciliation is a two-way street. For there were things I did to hurt my father. If only this reconciliation could have happened while he was alive! Still, I could be assured that in God, Papa had seen all of our story in perfect light, and his forgiveness was already there, waiting for me to receive it. If I am writing this book about the Father's embrace, it is because of the transformation that healing prayer has worked in me. Not that I know fully what that embrace means, but I know what it is to be delivered from the pain of unhealed memories and the clutch of unforgiveness.

Forgiving your father? Forgiving your mother? How about your spouse or your brother or sister or that employer who fired you or blamed you for what someone else did? Or that person who injured or killed your child? Though parental relationships are the deepest, forgiveness is not limited to them. In the prayer to "Our Father," we ask to be forgiven, promising to forgive others, and that means anyone who has hurt us. There is no limitation. Jesus tells us to love even our enemies.

How can that be if justice is not served? Justice, yes, but not recrimination, not retaliation. It does not mean we have to say that what that person did was right. If it was right, we don't need to forgive. No, it was wrong. But what good does it do to hang on to our bitterness, our grudge, our resentment? It is in our own interest that we need to forgive. Recently, the news media carried the story of a survivor of the Holocaust who, having lived for decades in hatred of the Nazis, said she chose to forgive, not for their sake, but for hers. She said the Holocaust was torture enough; she didn't need the continuing torture of hatred. As one old rancher quoted to me: "Hatred, like acid, eats the containing vessel."

But Jesus gives a different reason for forgiveness and love of our enemies: "That you may be children of your heavenly Father"

(Matthew 5:45). Children bear the genes of their parents. Christians bear in their hearts the genes of their heavenly Father. Jesus shared the same divine nature as his heavenly Father, and so he forgave his enemies from the cross. We do not become God, of course, but we share in Jesus' relationship with the Father when, like Jesus, we are held close to the Father's heart in the divine embrace. We are too close to the furnace of all love to hold the ice of hate. Forgiveness must be part of our new nature as God's children. Forgive because God forgives. You are God's child.

And God has forgiven you. That is the second reason Jesus gives for forgiving. But that deserves a separate chapter.

....

Jesus, from the cross you gave the supreme example: "Father, forgive them, for they do not know what they are doing" (Luke 23:34, my translation). I kneel at the foot of your cross, asking you to reveal to me anyone I have not forgiven. I know it is only with your grace that I can forgive. But with your grace, I will. Amen.

FOR REFLECTION

1. Do you have any story from your life that is similar to (or maybe contrasts with) the story of Fr. George's father?

2. Why is forgiveness so key to healing the father wound?

3. Do you still have unresolved issues with your father? How can forgiveness help you to resolve them?

CHAPTER 5

Healing the Father Wound, Part II

When is the time for healing the father wound? When one becomes aware of it. Sometimes soldiers are grazed by a bullet and don't even realize they've been hit until they discover a good deal of blood. A nurse friend of mine was right behind the young leader of a march for peace in Ireland when a shot rang out, killing him and grazing my friend's arm. When she returned to the States, she gradually became ill from the bullet's poison and needed medical intervention. So too with many of us. We may carry the father wound well into adulthood before we realize we are bleeding from it. Or poisoned by it. That's why many experience the healing process only later in their lives.

But children can sometimes be graced with insight that leads to their healing early in life. I want to share with you two stories of children of a single mother who were savagely abused by their father but in childhood were already beginning to heal. The following stories, as related by their mother, are true. I asked her to write them out because of the amazing grace these children experienced at an early age. I have only changed their names to protect their privacy.

As background, I must tell you that the father, whom we will call Hank, had sexually abused his five-year-old daughter, Jennifer.

This, with other abuses, not only led to her parents' divorce but to a restraining order that he might see his children, Jennifer and younger brother, Peter, only with another adult present. In fact, his contact now has become minimal, apparently by his own choice. Here in italics are the children's stories, as related by their mother:

Because of the sexual abuse that my daughter, Jennifer, has suffered, I have been working with her through play therapy. A psychologist is teaching me how to truly listen to her and facilitate the healing/therapeutic process. What she said to me one day was truly amazing and shows what tremendous healing she is experiencing.

Peter, my three-year-old, had fallen asleep in the car as I was driving home from picking up Jennifer from kindergarten. Arriving home, I put Peter in bed and spent this therapeutic one-on-one time with her. We played for an hour and it was simply fun; nothing truly therapeutic surfaced. Then we continued to play together over dinner. And as we sat down at our table to eat, we continued our play with My Little Pony toys. Then she told me, "The mama horse was in a war, a battle fighting for her children. The mama horse was supposed to be at home, cuddling with her children, and the daddy horse was supposed to be fighting for them." Then she took the baby horse and almost whispered to her, "Your daddy was there at the wedding, but then he left. But don't worry. Because God was with you, Jesus was with you, the Dove was with you, and the Lady was with you. He took something good from inside of you. But the Father put it back."

Of course, here she is referring not only to the sexual abuse and her innocence, but also to the tremendous battle that was forged by my efforts and my family's efforts to gain full and total custody of the children to protect them from Hank. Thanks be to God, because the victory is the Lord's.

Another thing that Jennifer told me, which she just spontaneously said: "Sometimes I picture God and Jesus." Surprised, I asked her what she thought God looks like. And she said, "He is young and pretty and huge. And when he holds us in his hands, we become as big as he is." This is a tremendous indication that she feels the awesome protection of God's power, something most victims of sexual abuse, or of any abuse, fail to experience. This is a sure sign that God is moving her out of victimhood into restored dignity.

My son, Peter, has also experienced healing through the love of our Father. A few weeks ago, I was putting on his shoes as we sat on the couch in our living room. He asked me, squirming a little as I fastened the Velcro, "Where is my dad?" Hank has not been present to either of them for almost two and a half years now. He sporadically comes in and out of their lives, usually for only a day or two at a time. The time between his visits or phone calls ranges from six weeks to three months. Thus, he not only abused Jennifer, but he has since orphaned both of them. So with deep sorrow in my heart, I proceeded to tell Peter the truth about his father and the truth about his God, the same statements I repeat to them almost every day: "Your dad is not here. He lives in Houston and is working. He has chosen not to be with us. But you have a heavenly Father who is always with you. And He loves you." Peter leaned back—all the way back into the recesses of the couch—and said with a huge grin, and almost in a giggle, "And he loves to kiss me! And I love to kiss him!"

We don't know what flashbacks these children will have in adulthood, but they have been equipped with tools that, with God's grace, will enable them to lead wholesome lives without bleeding from the father wound. In fact, their understanding of God the Father actually helped to start the healing process. Much of this help has come from their mother's teaching them about the nature of God. Jennifer's image of God the Father, far from chafing the pain she suffered from her earthly father, actually became a healing balm for her. And when held by God or Jesus, "we become as big as he is." Even a child can feel the strength of his giant God. Peter's understanding of God's fatherly love has helped him to cope with the absence of his earthly father.

May none of us limp through life nursing a father wound and inflicting it on others. There is healing, victory, and new life in the fatherhood of God.

....

Father, whatever my age, I do not want to carry wounds, recent or ancient, that keep me from experiencing the spiritual freedom you want to give me. You want me to be whole. Because I am not, I sometimes inflict my woundedness on others who were in no way the cause of my hurt. I want to become "as big as you are" by forgiving as you do. Jesus, forgiving your enemies from the cross, help me to do the same. Amen.

For Reflection

1. Which childhood experiences strengthened your bond with your father? Which ones weakened it?

2. If you have had a father wound, did it affect your behavior with others? How so?

3. If you have had a father wound, when did you become actively aware of it? Are you aware of a father wound in someone close to you? How can you help that person begin the healing process?

CHAPTER 6

Wounds of Spouses and Peers

In the previous two chapters, I have talked about the father wound and the beauty and the freedom of forgiving and setting our parent—and ourselves—free. But that is not the only kind of hurt we may receive in life. Our woundedness may come from anyone, most frequently from spouses or peers. No matter what the source, unforgiveness of any kind will block intimacy with the Father, for Jesus says, "Be merciful, just as your Father is merciful" (Luke 6:36).

This theme of the relationship between our forgiveness and the Father's forgiveness appears most often in the Gospel of Matthew. The prayer that Jesus taught us sits enthroned in the center of the Sermon on the Mount, and in that prayer we say, "Forgive us our trespasses *as we forgive* those who have trespassed against us" (the liturgy's translation of Matthew 6:12, emphasis mine). As if that weren't enough, in case we missed it, Jesus adds, "If you forgive others their transgressions, your heavenly Father will forgive you. But if you do not forgive others, neither will your Father forgive your transgressions" (Matthew 6:14-15).

This central teaching of Jesus is beautifully portrayed in the parable of the unforgiving debtor (Matthew 18:21-35). It would be worth your while to pause here and read it from your Bible.

A servant owes his master ten thousand talents. (How he managed to amass that galactic debt is left for us to imagine.) The master orders him, with his family and property, to be sold *toward* payment of the debt, which is so great that it really can't be paid. Aware of the impossibility, still the servant asks for time: "Please just extend the note; give me a little more time, and I'll pay it back in full." At this point, the master is moved with compassion. He does not give the debtor time; instead, he forgives the entire debt.

Obviously, this is no human creditor; it is our foolishly compassionate God. Because the debt stands for the guilt we have amassed through our sins against God (the one quasi-"infinite" thing we humans can do), it takes God to forgive the debt. And he does. But unmoved by the forgiveness that he has received, the debtor then throttles a fellow servant who owes him a pittance and demands that he pay it immediately. When he cannot pay, the forgiven debtor has his fellow servant thrown into prison until he can pay the debt. The master explodes in anger, and amazingly, the identity of the master is revealed. He is your "Father" (Matthew 18:35). Nowhere in the Gospels is this infinitely compassionate Father angrier than at this moment. He hands the forgiven servant over to the torturers until he pays the whole debt.

Note the sentence is not jail time—it is torture. At the spiritual level, this is exactly what unforgiveness is: torture. It is not really God torturing me but torture of my own choosing. Thinking to imprison the other in my heart, it is I who am the prisoner—the prisoner of my own unforgiveness.

Trapped by Unforgiveness

After I had preached on this parable of the unforgiving servant, a woman approached me and said, "When my husband returned from Vietnam, he was a changed man. He was full of anger, and he took it out on me. He once struck me on the head right where my bobby pin was. That was terribly painful. I was so angry that I took the bobby pin and stuck it in a crack of the wall next to the refrigerator, where I could remember it every day. Every day for twenty-seven years! But, Father, the word of God has convicted me. When I go home, I'm throwing that bobby pin away and forgiving my husband."

Twenty-seven years of torture. What a pity, and what deadly torture! The fact is that many of us can carry that kind of torture for years, perhaps in a dungeon so deep that we have thrown away the key. In the days of black-and-white movies, there was a documentary in which animal collector Frank Buck was trying to capture a particular type of monkey in Africa for zoos in the United States. He was having a very difficult time, for the monkeys were wily. After several failures, he finally found that the monkeys loved rice. So he drilled small holes into coconuts staked to the ground and filled them with rice. When the monkeys inserted their paws and grabbed a handful of rice, they could not get their paws out. Unfailingly, all the monkeys were captured because they would not let go of the rice! That's the way it is with unforgiveness. We won't let go, and we are trapped.

Letting go not only sets us free. It lets the Father embrace us.

Forgiveness also removes the blocks for healing. Eric Espinoza was watching television in his family's living room. The thirteen-year-old, who had never been involved with drugs or gangs, suddenly slumped, struck in the head by a drive-by shooter who had aimed at the wrong house. Eric was near death. Rushed to the hospital, he lay unconscious and motionless in a bed as his family gathered around him. Monique, herself a teenaged friend and a member of our prayer group, took the initiative to lead them in prayer. She could sense anger and bitterness in the family. "We cannot expect healing unless we forgive the one responsible," she said. They prayed. No sign of improvement from Eric, still unconscious, his body still as death. Boldly, Monique demanded, "Is there anyone here who hasn't forgiven?" Eric's aunt admitted that she was locked in unforgiveness. More prayer, this time for her. Finally, she sighed, "I forgive." At that moment, Eric moved for the first time, the beginning of his healing. Eric went on to play football for his high school.

"Does anyone nourish anger against another / and expect healing from the LORD?" (Sirach 28:3). The healing the Father wanted was more than Eric's. He wanted to heal the family by giving them a taste of his own forgiving love.

....

The ones we love are the ones who can hurt us the most. Father, whether they be my spouse, family members, friends, or co-workers, give me a larger heart, like the one you have shown in Jesus, which embodies your mercy and forgiveness. Amen.

FOR REFLECTION

1. Why is God's forgiveness of us inseparably linked to our forgiveness of others?

2. In praying with someone for physical healing, why would it be appropriate to ask the person if there is anyone they need to forgive?

3. In what way is forgiveness a foretaste of heaven?

CHAPTER 7

Pure Eyes, Pure Heart

I n 1992, five hundred years after Christopher Columbus brought the faith to the Western hemisphere, Jim Murphy decided to commemorate the event by carrying a cross from the first mission in St. Augustine, Florida, to the missions in California—on foot. Zigzagging across the country to visit all the missions along the way, he traveled forty-two hundred miles. When he arrived in San Antonio, he was desperately ill. It was my privilege to visit him in the convent that provided a *posada* for him, to pray with him and anoint him with the Sacrament of the Sick. Later, he told me the following story, which he has given me permission to share.

One day as Jim was bearing the cross along a back road in the Texas panhandle, his eyes fell on a magazine that someone had tossed on the roadside. There, a pornographic image of a young woman beckoned to him. Tired as he was, he instantly felt the desire for a moment of sensual relief that he knew was also an invitation to lust. Struggling, he plodded on, swimming against a current of self-indulgence that all but overwhelmed him. Finally, relief came to him, not by turning back, but by hearing in the depths of his being one word: *Abba*. *Abba* told him that this woman had a daddy, a human daddy who loved her and would be shamed by that photo, and a heavenly *Abba* who saw in her his blood-bought daughter and the divine destiny for which he had created her, an *Abba* the girl did not know. Jim's cross grew lighter and his journey merrier as he pondered the power of that word. The word had transformed her in his heart from an object to be used into a person to be loved. Jim began to pray for her, hoping that one day he would meet her in heaven transformed in the holiness of the Father's glory.

Indeed, in the word "*Abba*" and the experience of the Holy Spirit that gives its meaning, the Father not only reveals himself. He also throws light on everything else, and particularly on man and woman, the crowning masterpiece of his creation. Not only is every human person, man or woman, made in the image and likeness of the Creator. In the light of revelation, human relationships also reflect something of the inner relationships of the Trinity. Not that they would suffice to prove by reason that the Trinity exists. But they are the best analogy we have for understanding what it is to be "Father," what it is to be begotten of him, and what the sigh of love between them might be.

And it is in terms of relationships illumined by the divine relationships that the challenge to purity exists. Pornography, as well as every other form of violence to women, wrests the woman from the totality of her being, including her relationships, and turns the partial in violence against the whole. It turns the sexual against the dignity of the person to whom the sexual belongs. And it attacks the relationships that are part of that dignity, be it the relationship to parent, to spouse, to children, or to God. Yes, God, for he is the ultimate guarantor of the person's dignity and destiny, and the Father after whom all relationships are named

(Ephesians 3:15). That is why the embrace of the Father makes us see everyone in his light. We look into his eyes, as it were, and see there reflected not only ourselves but every other person. And to see them with his eyes is to see them with his love. They are precious in his eyes, and they become precious in ours. To violate them, if only in look or thought, is to trash the holy and taste the sweet poison of hell.

Seeing with the Father's Eyes

Jesus can help us to see with the Father's eyes. "Whoever has seen me has seen the Father," Jesus said (John 14:9), and that means that in his humanity, we can see exactly what the Father is like as well as what the ideal son or daughter of the Father should be like. In that sense, Jesus *is* the kingdom of God on earth.

But Jesus does not exist in isolation, without his being in relationship with others; that is why we can't understand Jesus if we don't look also at his relationships. Of course, his essential relationship is with his Father in heaven and with the Holy Spirit, by whom he was conceived and anointed for his ministry and, ultimately, for his saving death and resurrection. But we learn from his human relationships how to relate with those among whom we find ourselves. His first human relationship was with his mother. It was the closest, most intimate of his human relationships. True, one day in his teaching, he showed the superiority of the relation of faith to that of the flesh, be it even the holiest flesh of his mother. But she, too, surpassed even her own exceptional physical role by the role of her faith, as Jesus made clear when the woman in the crowd praised the womb and breasts of Jesus' mother: "Rather, blessed are those who hear the word of God and observe it" (Luke 11:28), for that is what she did (1:38).

We could look at all his other relationships noted in the Gospels, but in this chapter on purity, we look at Jesus' relationship with women. On the one hand, he shocks his contemporaries by his disregard for some of the barriers in his Jewish culture. He begins a conversation with a woman who is not his wife, and he discusses her marital affairs (John 4:4-30). He allows a woman known to be a sinner to wash his feet with her tears—to the shock of his Pharisee host (Luke 7:36-50). He has in his retinue of disciples a woman out of whom he has cast seven devils (Luke 8:1-3), and in his resurrection, he appears first to her (John 20:11-18). And he is hosted at a meal by two women (Luke 10:38-42). And yet, in all of these, there is no whiff of self-interest but, rather, the upholding of their dignity and destiny. We see this in the story of the Samaritan woman and especially in his defense of the woman caught in adultery, to whom he says only, "Neither do I condemn you. Go, [and] from now on do not sin any more" (John 8:11). And we may presume that he is the first to give the example of his teaching: "Everyone who looks at a woman with lust has already committed adultery with her in his heart" (Matthew 5:28).

Jesus' inner freedom in his love for men and women proceeded from his own resting in the Father's embrace. He was celibate, but he also knew that the love of married couples is blessed, for in their faithful, committed love, they reflect the undying embrace of the Father's love. So too, women who live in *Abba's* embrace, whether in the memory of their human father or in the embrace of God's fatherly love, know their dignity and their destiny in a way that the girl in the roadside photo unfortunately did not. And to them, to think of showing even a slight immodesty that might invite lust would not even occur. Filled with love and feeling no need to kindle passion, they wish to reflect the Father's glory in the total beauty of their lives. The beauty of a holy woman captivates the human heart in a way that lust does not. It captivated the heart of God, who chose the most beautiful, because the holiest, as his mother.

....

Father, I am very aware that I still feel the effects of original sin in the pulls of the flesh. Temptation offers me a distorted view of others. If only I could see them with your eyes and your heart and the eyes and heart of Jesus and Mary. Please grant me the grace to do so. Amen.

For Reflection

1. How did the thought of *Abba* help Jim to overcome his temptation to lust?

2. How was Jesus' own respect for women shaped by the love and example of his own mother?

3. Is it true that "the beauty of a holy woman captivates the human heart in a way that lust does not"? Can you think of women of whom this is strikingly true? Of men?

CHAPTER 8

Asleep in
the Storm

W hat in the name of heaven is going on?" Startled
by sirens and shouts, I swung out of my bed and
peered out the window into the school yard, where
two fire trucks and several police cars were flashing their lights.
A TV camera focused on my pajama-clad form, the first person
visible in the Marianist residence.

Fortunately, it was only a minor bedroom blaze, already
doused by home extinguishers. But the night was not over. Fire-
fighters with cleated boots stomped up the three flights of stairs
to check out the site and to set up roaring fans to blow out the
smoke. Like myself, the other brothers poured out of their bed-
rooms to see the spectacle—all but one, the brother directly across
from the fire, who slept through it all and at breakfast accused us
of inventing a spoof. How could anyone directly across the hall
from the shouting and the clatter sleep through it all?

It was not the first time that someone had slept through a
storm. Jesus would have slept through the lashing waves and
wind had not his fear-stricken disciples staggered their way to the
back of the boat and roused him. In their panic, they even implied
that he had chosen to sleep while they despaired of surviving.
"Teacher, do you not care that we are perishing?" (Mark 4:38). In

Mark's version, Jesus rebukes the disciples for their lack of faith *after* he calms the storm. But Matthew tells us that Jesus rebukes them *before* stilling the storm: "Why are you terrified, O you of little faith?" (8:26). The implication is this: "If you had faith, you would not have wakened me; you would have trusted that your Father would care for you." Matthew's placing of Jesus' rebuke before he stills the storm, rather than after, teaches us a lesson: it is easy to have faith once the storm is stilled; the challenge is to have faith in the midst of the storm. Jesus had no fear, for he was sleeping in the Father's embrace. However we interpret the story, Jesus is inviting us to trust the Father no matter what the circumstances, and to trust him when we are in the midst of the storm.

We may not be at sea when the storm breaks; we might be in the comfort of our home. That's where I was when the phone rang with the news that my beautiful twenty-five-year-old niece had just been killed when an eighteen-wheeler crushed her car. The storm might be like the shock of a woman I know, whose husband and father of their six children walked out on them to marry another. Storms because of finances or illness or natural disasters or the collapse of two Manhattan towers—all of these challenge us who believe in a loving Father. Why are these things happening to us, we ask. And we may even get angry with God and blame him, saying with Job, "If it is not he, who then is it?" (9:24). Logic can tell us that good is greater than evil; that it is the nature of material things, even our bodies, to collide; that moral evil is due to man's abuse of God-given free will. But in the anguish of the moment, we do not think logically. We do not think at all—we feel. Can we believe, can we trust *in* the storm?

Can we believe that God is really *Abba*? Can we believe that he is truly there? Is he still holding us in his embrace?

Not Understanding but Believing

We are not the first to whom those questions come. There was a woman standing in grief before her crucified son, a woman who, more than any, had a right to ask those questions. Children are not supposed to die before their parents, yet it happens all the time. But the death of this woman's son is neither the result of illness nor accident. It is the horrendous result of betrayal, rejection, and abandonment. The blood that drips from his wounds is blood given him from her womb. How could he, the most innocent of men, die the death of a criminal? He whose hands had only healed and blessed—those hands, now nailed to a cross?

Yet she stood. Not understanding but believing. Believing that God makes all things work together unto good for those who love him (Romans 8:28), though she saw not clearly how. Even in his agony, Jesus rests on the Father's breast, saying, "Father, into your hands I commend my spirit" (Luke 23:46), and when he falls asleep in death, God brings from his wounded side, as from the new Adam, his bride, the Church. Does Mary see all this? No, for she walks by faith and not by sight (2 Corinthians 5:7), just as grieving and storm-tossed Christians believe in the redemptive power of their own suffering if joined to his (Colossians 1:24).

So we are not alone. A compassionate, suffering mother enables us to live with the question when we don't see the answer. She believes and trusts that at this moment, more than ever, her dying son is held in his Father's embrace. And in her faith, she, too, is held in that embrace. The surface may be turmoil, but her depth is anchored in peace. No matter the storm, at her side we, too, can know the Father's embrace. Humanly it seems to make no sense.

No more than Jesus sleeping in the storm.

....

Jesus, you once said you had nowhere to lay your head. But as your body was taken down from the cross, you finally laid it where you had laid it as a child—at Mary's breast. In so doing, you showed us in time where you rest it for all eternity, on the Father's breast. When storms surround me, and especially when the hour of death approaches, may I rest with you on the Father's breast. Amen.

FOR REFLECTION

1. Recall a storm that you experienced at some time in your life. How did you handle it? What resources did you seek?

2. Do you recall a time when you were able to have inner peace in the midst of suffering?

3. Have you found in Mary a support in times of turmoil, grief, and chaos?

CHAPTER 9

Papa, You're
Too Big!

"Papa, you're too big!" At the age of five, I was struggling to get my arms around my father's fifty-five-inch waist. It was a game we played periodically to measure my growth against his enormous belly. I could reach up and touch him, but I could not get my arms all the way around him.

That's the way it is with our words about God. The human words God has used to reveal himself allow us to touch him. But none of our words can contain him. Words are limited; God is not.

For example, when we call God "Father," we are affirming a truth, since Jesus used that word to tell us who God is. And if the Holy Spirit gives us the *experience* of *Abba,* that, too, is touching God. It is true, it is possible for the creature to experience the mystery, for St. Paul tells us that the Holy Spirit bears united witness with our spirit that we are the children of God, and the Spirit is the one who cries *"Abba"* in our hearts (Galatians 4:6). And yet neither the word nor the experience totally contains God; we can't just put him in a box and figure him out. What is beyond our touching infinitely surpasses what we touch. What we don't know about God, even when we call him *Abba,* is much greater than what we do know. That doesn't mean our understanding is false; it is just inadequate. But it's all we've got. It is part of the revelation, though, that we have touched the frontier of a limit-less beyond.

How do we live with that?

First of all, we live it in prayer. Our first real experience of God as Father can be electrifying. After I was prayed over for what charismatics call the "baptism in the Holy Spirit," I experienced God as my father in a way I never had before. That sustained me for many years, until I began to wonder whether it was really God I was experiencing or only my own experience. There is a whole philosophical issue involved here that need not detain us. Suffice it to say that the philosopher Immanuel Kant and many who have followed him have maintained that we never know the real world but only our concepts of the real world. Not so. Our concepts are not *what* we know but that *by which* we know the real world. It is *through* our experience that we contact reality. But it is reality that we contact.

However, in the spiritual life, when we are talking about know-ing God in faith, the soul reaches a point at which it feels more dissatisfaction than satisfaction with its experience of God. It may even wonder whether it is really experiencing God at all. It may fear Kant was right. That is frightening to a soul that has lived in the assumption that it was in loving, filial contact with a God it has known as "Father." The reality is that it is discovering not the deception but simply the limits of the knowledge of God in this life. Even the highest mystical knowledge is not the beatific vision. The inadequacy that the soul feels with its own experience points to the limitless unknown. It had lived a world of horizons and limits; now it is lost, untethered in space.

And yet not untethered. For there is one remaining cord: faith. The soul is reaching what theologians call the "apophatic" dimension of God's self-revelation. God is both like and unlike the best of human fathers. Like, because he has chosen human fatherhood as the primary metaphor for the caring, self-sacrificing love that he is. Unlike, because he has none of the limitations of human fatherhood. He is Father—*and so much more.* Papa, you're too big! Yes, I'm touching you, but I'll never get my arms all the way around you. But I can live with that because in faith, I know *your* arms are all the way around *me.* Even when I don't feel it.

So much for prayer. What about when we take up our daily routine, driving to work, sweating out a deadline [instead of "sweating," I first mistakenly typed "swearing"], shopping for groceries, going to the movies, eating lunch or dinner, interacting with loved ones or co-workers? Does the "beyond-ness" of God have anything to do with that?

At first sight, it might seem not. If, in the busyness of my day, I have a hard time remembering the consoling presence of my *Abba,* how can I survive when I come to realize how inadequate even my image of the Father is? Our solution is not to go higher in speculation but to come down to earth and seek the wisdom of children. We turn to Jennifer, the little girl who was abused by her father. When she talked of God the Father, she said, "He is huge, and when he holds us in his hands, we become as big as he is." The hugeness of the Father, the fact that he is bigger than we can imagine, empowers us in a way that even the best of human fathers cannot. We become "as big as he is," not by becoming God, but by experiencing the power of the Father *almighty.* The "beyond-ness" of God does not empty "Father" of all we have known of him but fills it with infinite life and power. And that fills us with unspeakable boldness. "With my God to help I can leap a wall" (Psalm 18:30).

The key for us, as it was for Jennifer, is not trying to encompass the infinite Father with our puny minds but allowing him to encompass us. "When *he* holds us in *his* hands." That, of course, is the fruit of faith. We need to let him do it. And when we do, we know a love we have never known before. We are afloat in an infinite ocean. We are held in infinite hands, yet hands that hold us as if we were the only one in the world, the hands of a father holding his newborn child.

Papa, my arms can't reach around you, but your arms reach around me. And that is enough—for now.

....

Father, you go beyond all that my mind can grasp. When my mind falters at the frontier of infinity, reassure me that you are holding me. And while I long for your ultimate embrace in heaven, until we meet face-to-face, may I rest in your hands with the trust of a child. Amen.

For Reflection

1. Why is the infinity of God not something to inspire fear but rather confidence?

2. In what sense can Jennifer be right when she says, "When he holds us in his hands, we become as big as he is"?

3. Have you ever experienced the power of the Father *almighty*? What was it like?

CHAPTER 10

The Name, the Kingdom, the Will

Contemplation and intercession: these were the two effects of the Holy Spirit that we saw in chapter 3. Contemplation of the limitless wonder of God who, despite his complete otherness and infinite distance in being, nevertheless comes to us as *Abba*, our dearest Father. Intercession, because the same Holy Spirit who shows us the Person of the Father impels us to pray for the coming of his kingdom. It is no surprise, then, that in the Lord's Prayer, after addressing *Abba*, we should find ourselves praying for the completion of God's kingdom on earth. The first invocation, "Hallowed be thy name," is a praise of God, telling us that praise should be the first thing we say to God, yet this invocation is already an intercessory prayer.

How so? We must first be aware that in Hebrew, a verb in the passive voice is often what the grammarians call a "divine passive," so that in our case, "Hallowed be thy name" would be a respectful way of saying, "Hallow thy name," meaning here, "Show the holiness of your name." This is the meaning we find in the Book of Ezekiel, when the Lord says that although his people have desecrated his name among the Gentiles, he will show the holiness of his name by doing something for them, namely by gathering his people and bringing them home to their land:

> Not for your sake do I act . . . but for the sake of my holy name,
> which you desecrated among the nations. . . . But I will show
> the holiness of my great name . . . when through you I show
> my holiness before their very eyes. I will take you away from
> among the nations, gather you from all the lands, and bring
> you back to your own soil. I will sprinkle clean water over you
> to make you clean; from all your impurities and from all your
> idols I will cleanse you. I will give you a new heart, and a new
> spirit I will put within you. (Ezekiel 36:22-26)

In other words, God shows the holiness of his name by acting on the stage of history, saving his people from their slavery and exile. So here we, too, are asking the Father to show the holiness of his name, that is, to show that his name is not a tag for a distant and uncaring God but an infinite power waiting to be deployed. The comfort that we find in the Father's embrace is thus also a trust that he will act when we are in need, and like children, we should not hesitate to ask. But the something for which we primarily ask for here is the coming of God's kingdom rather than our own. We pray for our Father's glory first. There is really no risk in that. Rather, it is the best way, for if we seek God's kingdom first, everything else will be given us besides (Mathew 6:33).

Thus, "Hallowed be thy name" comes close to the next invocation, "Thy kingdom come." It would be worth the experience to ask a Bible-study or faith-sharing group what they understand by this invocation. Some would probably say that they are praying to get into the kingdom of heaven. Others might say they are asking for God's kingdom to come on earth. The latter folks would be right. For like the preceding invocation, this one prays for something to happen in this world. God has a blueprint for the human race, and Christ and his Church have the truth and the power to bring it about if the human race would cooperate. It is the kingdom of which God is the supreme authority, for he is the King.

"My Father, the King"

Notice how the Lord's Prayer tells us that our Father is also King. That image complements the tenderness in the title "*Abba,*" for it conveys security to the child of God, knowing that the Father has power and authority to rule and protect. One would think that five-year-old Jennifer, sexually abused by her father, would have a hard time thinking of God as her father, for I know many adults who have struggled with that kind of memory for years. But amazingly, this little child knows the difference between the hideous ogre she has to call "father" and God, whom she calls "my Father, the King."

Since Jesus wants us to pray, "Thy kingdom come," he is giving us a responsibility for bringing it about. We do that, first of all, by our intercession. But implied also is our action. In places where Christians are hounded and persecuted, there is often nothing more they can do but witness by their fidelity. But where they enjoy freedom, as we still do in this country, there are wide avenues for promoting justice and living charity. Indeed, those whom Jesus calls into the kingdom of heaven are those who have fed the hungry, clothed the naked, and done other works of mercy to promote the kingdom on earth.

Finally, we pray, "Thy will be done on earth as it is in heaven." The common understanding of this phrase is that we accept whatever God sends us, especially if it was not what we wanted. But that is a much too hasty and personal interpretation of the words. The primary meaning is basically the same as the two previous petitions. It is an assertive prayer: "May your will, your plan of salvation for the world, be accomplished in our lifetime." That was certainly Jesus' prayer during his public ministry, and it was what Jesus told his disciples to pray for: "Dear Father, win the victory of your justice, your truth, your love. You are King—bring about your kingdom. Establish it where it is not."

Our striving is part of the struggle to bring that kingdom about. And in the process, we may also ask for our part to be achieved in the kingdom, and we may have a very good idea exactly what that should be, including the realization of our dreams. However, we also know that our world is filled with shattered dreams and broken promises. We expect our marriage to be heaven on earth, but our spouse dies young in an accident, or leaves us. We want to become a doctor to serve the poor, and we can't get into medical school. We have the ability to become an Olympian racer but ruin our back in an accident (this happened to one of my students). Jesus tried to convert his people, but confronted with deaf hearts and, ultimately, betrayal, he ended up on the cross instead. In the garden, faced with the apparent failure of his mission and his own horrible death, Jesus prayed the prayer he had taught his disciples: "Thy will be done." But now it meant surrender: "Not my will but thine be done."

When our dreams and even our prayers lead us rather to the cross, can we accept the failure of our Plan A and let God make a beautiful Plan B? Praying to the Father in the power of the Holy Spirit can change our little Good Fridays into Easter Sundays.

"Thy will be done," begun as intercession, becomes surrender. And surrender becomes God's new tool for the kingdom, just as Jesus' surrender in the garden of Gethsemane, renewed on the cross, opened the garden of Paradise for all of us good thieves.

....

Father, I pray for the coming of your kingdom—in my life, in the life of my family, in my church, and in my world. When my dreams are shattered, please pick up the pieces and show me how to find peace, meaning, and mission for my life in a Plan B. And may that plan become part of your bringing about your kingdom in this world. Amen.

FOR REFLECTION

1. In what way is calling God "our Father" really a call to action on our part?

2. Do you consider intercession for others and for the world a necessary consequence of calling God "Father"?

3. In your life, have you experienced the failure of a Plan A? If so, how are you allowing the Father to help you make a beautiful Plan B?

CHAPTER 11

Bread for His Children

In Victor Hugo's *Les Misérables*, the protagonist, Jean Valjean, steals a loaf of bread to feed his sister's seven starving children and is sent to prison for it. This is what launches the plot of one of the world's most famous novels—the story of a man who puts his future at risk for the sake of those who have no bread.

God the Father took the greatest risk of all when he saw his chosen people and the hoards of all mankind starving in the hunger pangs of sin, violence, and bloodshed. The risk? Sending his own Son to be their food. This was not like sending the manna in the desert. No risk in that. If anyone didn't like that food, they could starve—their choice. But this is God sending his Son. Did the Father take a risk?

Sometimes the way we talk about God's plan could imply that God took no risk. "God sent his son to die for us." That is a simple formula that could hide the complexity of the mystery, and indeed, it could hide the humanity of God. God was not the murderer of Jesus. But Jesus' death fit into the divine plan. How, then, do we understand the Father's role and man's role in this mystery? It has to do with risk.

The key lies in the parable of the wicked vineyard tenants (Mark 12:1-12). Here Jesus portrays not only the Father's love for his son but also the indefatigable trust he has in the goodness of those to whom he sends him. The owner of a vineyard has gone to a lot of trouble laying out the vineyard: he puts a hedge around it, digs a winepress, and then builds a watchtower to protect it. He lends it out to tenant farmers, and when harvest time comes, he sends a servant to collect the owner's share of the revenue. Not only do the tenants beat the servant and send him away empty-handed, but they do the same and worse to successive servants, and one of them they kill. The owner keeps trying, believing that somehow the tenants will repent. Finally, he decides to send his son: "He had one other to send, a beloved son. He sent him to them last of all, thinking, *They will respect my son.*' . . . They seized him and killed him, and threw him out of the vineyard" (12:6, 8; emphasis mine).

That little phrase, "They will respect my son," tells us a lot about the Father's heart. First of all, the one he sends is his son, his *beloved* son. No servant or slave, this one. The father in the parable cherishes his son so much that he cannot imagine that the receivers would reject him: "They will respect my son." Despite all the previous rejections, the father trusts that the tenants will receive the son. Given the previous history, though, the father's decision is fraught with risk. Trust always implies risk. If I hire a worker with a perfect résumé and stellar, faithful performance elsewhere, that is logic, not trust. But if I decide to give an ex-convict a chance and hire him, I am taking a serious risk, and that is real trust. That is what the father does here. The normal listener to this parable will say, "But God, this is utter stupidity.

After all they have done, you are a fool to send your Son—unless with an army to annihilate those wretches." The Father continues to believe that the sinner will find a nugget of goodness in his heart to say yes to grace. He is the God of a second chance—and a third, a fourth, and as many as are needed. He risks. He trusts. Those who never trust may never get hurt, but they will wither for their lack of love. Those who trust know they may get hurt, but it is worth the risk. Jesus trusted Judas. Had he not, there would be no cross on Calvary, but neither would we have known the world's greatest act of love and been set free by it.

To the father's sorrow and grief, the tenants kill the son. They give him no respectful funeral and throw his body out of the vineyard. This was the collapse of God the Father's Plan A. The prophets God sent to call the people to repentance were rejected and killed. And so was the Son, who, of course, is Jesus. It was obviously not the Father who killed his Son. Evil men did it.

The Love and Trust of the Father

What is so amazing about the Father here is both his love and his trust. His love, not only for his Son, but for those bound in sin, and that is all of us. His trust: he has given us free will, and he respects that gift so much that he will not take it away. He wants the kind of free response that creates a friendship, a relationship of love. He offers the gift of gifts, risking refusal but also hoping for nothing more on our part than acceptance of the gift. If the tenants had accepted the son, then apparently all the previous refusals would have been forgiven. Repentance at the preaching of Jesus would have sufficed. Alas, it was not to be.

But in the end, God wins. He has a Plan B, made precisely from man's rejection of Plan A. The stone rejected by the builders has become the cornerstone (Mark 12:10). The death of Jesus, administered by man, is precisely the sacrifice fulfilling all sacrifices and rendering them obsolete. For those who accept it, the blood of the Son wipes away all sin and makes them sons and daughters in the Son. Lest there be any doubt that this is so, God raises Jesus and makes him the foundation of the new people of God. The Father uses the very blasphemous execution of his Son to achieve his purposes.

But how do we enter into that mystery? By faith and Baptism, of course. But faith and Baptism put us on a path with a journey ahead of us, and for that, Jesus devised a way to feed us on our journey lest we faint along the way (Matthew 15:32). The food is Jesus himself. He himself is the bread come down from heaven (John 6:51), no longer a metaphor but his own Body and Blood, available to us because it is in the form of something we can eat and drink. It is the ultimate fruit of the risk that the Father took in sending his Son.

That is why we, at a distance of two millennia, can be at Calvary and at the empty tomb, for the Jesus we receive is the risen Lord, with wounds now glorious badges of his sacrifice. The Father sacrificed his Son only in the sense that he allowed sinful humanity to do so, yet he accepted that sacrifice as sufficient to redeem all the sins of the world. In every Communion, we relive the Father's gift of the Son, grateful that the Father took the risk of sending him, grateful for the trust the Father extended to us—which we answered with bloodied, guilt-ridden hands—but even more grateful for the incredible paradox that the very blood of Jesus that we shed has washed us clean and shown us the heart of God.

....

We pray, Lord, for our daily bread, the needs of our bodily life. But even more important, we pray for the bread of the kingdom, the bread of the Great Tomorrow, the bread of heaven given to us now in the Body and Blood of Jesus. Open my eyes to this treasure, prepared at such a cost and available to me every day. May my life be a constant Eucharist, broken and shared with other hungry children. Amen.

FOR REFLECTION

1. How does the parable of the wicked vinedressers clarify who is responsible for the death of Jesus?

2. What risk has God the Father taken with you? How has he shown his trust in you?

3. When have you experienced the Eucharist as food for your journey? How did it strengthen you?

CHAPTER 12

Father's Breast, Mother's Breast

No one has ever seen God. The only begotten Son, God, ever resting on the Father's breast, has revealed him" (John 1:18, my translation). Despite the few references in the Old Testament that an individual had seen God (Jacob—Genesis 32:31; Moses—Exodus 33:11; Isaiah in the Temple when the Lord called him to prophesy—Isaiah 6:5), these were visions and nothing more. "No one can see God and live" was the constant understanding of the people of God in the centuries before Jesus, and this is affirmed by John in the prologue of his Gospel. The one exception is the Son of God himself, as John tells us: Jesus can reveal the Father because he rests on the Father's breast. It is, of course, a metaphor, which is the best that human language can do to suggest the mystery of the intimate union of the Word with the Father, a union that precedes his appearing in the flesh of humanity.

While we cannot see the Father with our bodily eyes, or even with our souls in this life, Jesus reveals the Father to us by his life, his teachings, and his death and resurrection. Thus, John ends his prologue and introduces Jesus' public life with a curtain-raising climax: Jesus "has revealed him." And later, at the Last Supper, when Philip asks Jesus, "Show us the Father," Jesus replies, "Have

I been with you for so long a time and you still do not know me, Philip? Whoever has seen me has seen the Father" (John 14:8-9). Thus, just as we see the snowcapped mountain reflected in the lake beneath, so contemplating Jesus, we see what the Father is like in human terms.

But in the rush of scenes in the Gospels, from the manger in Bethlehem, to the Sermon on the Mount, to the cross on Calvary, Jesus moves so fast that it is not easy to see him *resting* on the Father's breast. There is, however, one scene that helps us understand. It happens in the first months of Jesus' life, a scene beloved of artists since the second century: the child on the breast of his mother.

Of course, there is nothing unique about a child resting on its mother's breast—we see it every day. But no mother-and-child scene can ever come close to Mary holding her child, for two reasons. First, she is the only parent, the only human source of this child, just as the Father is the only divine source. Hers is a celibate, virginal motherhood, as God's is a celibate fatherhood. Second, she is the actual collaborator in the mystery of his begetting in time. By the power of the Holy Spirit, the Word, proceeding from the Father in eternal generation, proceeds from the womb of Mary in temporal generation. And thus the Word becomes her son, enabling us to understand "Son" to be applied to the Trinitarian relationship of the Word to the Father.

Jesus, the Full Expression of the Father

This last aspect perhaps needs to be explained. We have come to know the mystery of God's intimate life, the Trinity, only through the revelation brought us by Jesus Christ. Neither he nor his Evangelists used the word "Trinity," but all the makings of the term are there in the New Testament. Jesus called God his Father, and so the early tradition and theological reflection began to speak of Jesus not only in time as the Son, but even to apply that title, "Son," to his eternal generation from the Father. That eternal generation so far surpasses the metaphor of "son" that another expression was used: the Word, indicating that he is the full expression of the first Person of the Trinity. That full expression can be called "generation" because the first Person "begets" the second in a way faintly like human beings beget their children. Unlike human generation, however, this begetting is a continual process, a continual generating action. So too the Word is continually being "spoken" by the Father, just as the Holy Spirit is constantly proceeding from the Father and the Son like a waterfall.

Now it was God's choice to let us have a peek into this mystery by sending his Word in the best expression he could think of: a human son. He did this, however, not through generation by a human father, but rather through a human mother, virginally, with the result that Jesus' eternal generation by the Father is not obscured but rather preserved and revealed. To put it briefly, we call the relationship between the first and second Persons of the Trinity a Father-Son relationship because the second Person appeared on earth as Son and, first of all, as son of Mary. Later, as an adult, he would speak of God as his Father and himself as the Son. But this revelation began when he became the son of Mary. Endowed with flesh from her, he could then speak to men of the Father from whom he proceeded in eternity as in time.

So when we see the child Jesus resting on the breast of his mother, if we look deeply enough, we also see Jesus resting on the breast of the Father. And we are invited to do the same, to rest with Jesus on the breast of the Father in love, total abandonment, and trust. And it may help to first think of ourselves as a child resting on Mary's breast, since that was the first step that Jesus took to show us the way to the Father. "I hold myself in quiet and silence, / like a little child in its mother's arms" (Psalm 131:2, NJB).

....

Lord Jesus, there is no scene that touches me with more tenderness than that of a mother holding her child at her breast. Thank you for choosing this scene as an icon of your resting on the breast of the Father, the relationship that you have chosen to share with me. May I know the Father's love more and more as you experience it so that I may reach the glory to which you have called me and bring others with me. Amen.

FOR REFLECTION

1. How does the image of the child Jesus resting on his mother's breast help us to understand Jesus, the eternal Word, resting on the Father's breast?

2. How does this image help us to realize that Mary is not an obstacle to understanding Jesus but part of the revelation of God himself?

3. Imagine yourself with Jesus, resting on the breast of your Father. Pray with this image for several minutes. What do you feel? What do you think Jesus, or the Father, might be saying to you?

CHAPTER 13

When the Father
<u>Takes Away</u>

"So you're mad at God?"

"Yes," my student said. "Why would he take my dad so young? And me, only eleven years old!"

"Well, you wouldn't be mad at him if you didn't believe in him," I offered.

I have lived this scene many times in my priestly ministry. I recall my phone waking me at 2:00 a.m. and one of my students weeping because he had just lost his grandma. He was Hispanic, and in Hispanic families, the grandmother is the wisdom figure and the cement of the extended family. This was especially true for my student, who was very close to his grandmother. Though startled that he should call me in the middle of the night, I felt strangely honored that he should look first to me and my fatherly shoulder to cry on.

How do we deal with grief? And how in grief do we deal with God? I decided to write this chapter the morning I happened upon a page from my journal written in Nepal nine years after my mother's death, in which I describe two dreams.

In the first dream, I was with my mother and my grandmother (who is also deceased) in the kitchen. Somehow, the question of their deaths arose, and at first I was frightened by the question.

Then I realized that *they* were accepting it as a matter of course and were not depressed by it. So I felt better myself, and I was somehow able to enter their experience, and I said to my mother, "Mama, the greatest thing you've ever taught me is that life is a series of holding on and letting go." She smiled as she opened the oven and said, "Yes, and the worst thing you can do is to hold on when it's time to let go."

In the next dream, I was walking in the courtyard of my alma mater, Central Catholic High School in San Antonio, and a seminary friend appeared. I said to him, "Did you know that Fr. Vasey died?" (Fr. Vasey was my teacher and the seminary rector.) My friend seemed completely unconcerned and replied in an almost flippant manner that we shouldn't grieve because Fr. Vasey was in heaven. I was angered because he seemed to be robbing me of the grief I was feeling—or at least the right to it.

When I shared these two dreams with my spiritual director, he noted how significant an influence my mother had on my life, and he asked whether I had really let go of her. The question surprised me, but it led to some deep probing, in prayer, of the meanings of those two dreams. Here is what I wrote in my journal at the time:

I am beginning to realize that the grieving process, in a faith context, has three moments, all described by Job: "The LORD gave and the LORD has taken away; / blessed be the name of the LORD" (1:21).

Stage One: "The LORD gave." With Mama, I certainly experienced this. After Jesus and grace, she was the very best gift the Lord gave to me. To realize that she was gift is already in some way to let go, because it gets beyond the demanding or "taking for granted" stage.

Stage Two: "The LORD has taken away." Grief is the experience of loss, but not just the way one might lose a book or a coat. It's a wrenching, a robbery, a theft. Someone has *taken* the beloved. As Mary Magdalene said, "They have taken the Lord from the tomb, and we don't know where they put him" (John 20:2). In the case of the *death* of the beloved, one is confronted sooner or later with the question of God—and one cannot escape the conclusion that if God is truly master of life and death, then it is *he* who has taken the beloved away. "If it is not he, who then is it?" (Job 9:24). The beloved has been wrenched from our hands, and the Lord is responsible. With Mama's death, I think my looking the Lord in the face about his taking her away is something I suppressed or postponed as unthinkable hubris. But if the *gift* of Mama is an unexplainable mystery, so is the loss of her—and the question of God must be faced—or the question to God must be put. No wonder some people turn their grief into anger at God.

Stage Three: "Blessed be the name of the LORD." This stage in my grief about Mama has been very vague—experienced intellectually, perhaps. On the level of the heart, I could praise him for the *gift* of her, but how could I praise him for taking her away? Wouldn't that be to deny the gift that she was? We praise God for taking away bad things. How could we praise him for taking something, someone so good?

Ah, yes, there are times when we rejoice that another has taken what is very precious to us. And that is when we give that precious thing or person to the other as *gift*. We rejoice when the gift has been accepted.

There is the truth of the present moment. Nine years after Mama's death, I can say I never consciously *gave* Mama back to the Lord. I'm still living in the pain of her being taken.

If I want to give the Lord something, surely she is the best gift I could give, other than my own life. In a sense, though, what is my own life if not in great part at least what has been given to me through the love of others, especially Mama's? So perhaps the first step in giving my life back to the Lord is to freely and consciously give him Mama.

But wasn't that done when I first left home at the age of fifteen? No, because in the adolescent assumption that mothers live forever, I didn't realize the gift she was, how much a part of my life she had become, how much of her I would actually carry with me even when physically separated from her. So the moment of truth about the complete letting go of her is now upon me—but this time, letting her go as I let go of a gift I want to give and that I want the Receiver to accept.

Yet what does the Lord get out of this gift? Why should he find it preferable that he have her in a way that he didn't have her when I had her too? The only thing that makes sense is that she might be with him in a way that she was not while with me. And that is a matter of faith, of course. But it must also be true that my giving her to him is also important to him, perhaps as important as her being with him.

And so, Lord, for her sake, for yours and for mine, I ask for the grace to say with all my heart, "Father, thank you for Mama. Thank you for giving her to me. Thank you for taking her to yourself. I forgive you for taking her before I had really given her to you. But I acknowledge that you are God, and it's not my role to tell you what to do. You are the God of the taking as well as the God of the giving. But now in the awesome freedom you have given me, the freedom you treasure so much, the freedom that dignifies me with your divine likeness, the freedom that can give birth to a gift that would delight you, I surrender: *I give Mama to you.* She was the best I had, and only you are worthy to receive this, my gift to you. I rejoice that you now have her. I have not lost her after all. I have given her to you." (If my favorite painting were stolen from me, I would lose it. But if I give it to someone, the painting has achieved its noblest vocation, to be the expression of love.)

Now I realize too that what made Stage Two so long before the appearance of Stage Three was that I never consciously gave Mama to the Lord before he took her. This raises the question of all my other loves and relationships and things—and finally my own life. My God, what an agenda!

To give the ones we love back to God is, in the final analysis, to love them as they truly are. For they, like us, are from God and for God. This appears so clearly as death approaches. There is nothing so cruel for the beloved one who is dying to feel as if he is betraying the survivors by leaving them. Thus, the last act of love that we can do for the dying is to give them permission to leave. In so doing, we are simply accepting and affirming who they are, who we are, and who God is. It is to love them as they truly are. What has made us fall in love with them is the divine enfleshed in them. That doesn't mean that they are only appearances or that our love for them is not real. But what it does mean is that it is a real grace of illumination to realize, in the real dynamics of loving, that the other is *gift,* a gift to which we have no right, and the *Giver* is *God.* To realize that, and to hold the other with a relaxed grasp, indeed, as one would hold the chalice of Christ's Blood, received from the Father and now totally returned to him—that is a great grace. For it frees us not only of possessiveness but frees the other to be what he or she truly is.

Does it mean there will never be grieving when the beloved is taken by the Father? No. Jesus wept at the tomb of Lazarus. But somehow I feel that putting our loved ones back in the hands of the Father relieves them of the expectation of being God, and we can enjoy the gift of others in a contemplative way, freed from an excessive anxiety that we will lose the beloved. For in faith, when the Lord takes the beloved, their life's purpose is fulfilled.

Do I really believe that? Can I really rejoice that Mama is with the Lord and say, "Lord, in your wisdom, you took her at the time you chose"? I feel the loss, but I now surrender her as the best gift I can give him. And I ask for the grace to hold each of my loved ones gently, reverently, and to offer them each to God, their author and their end, and thus to love them as they truly are— and to discover that I've really not lost them but found them, as if for the first time, in that gifted radiance in which they truly are.

And that is heaven already begun here below. For heaven is our love brought to its perfection, rid of all the impurities of earthly love. And the purification process has begun even now. I don't lose the ones I love but find oneness with them at a new, surprising, and truer depth. One never really loses what one gives to God.

....

Lord Jesus, you wept at the tomb of Lazarus. You know what loss is and what grieving is. You used your power to bring your friend back to life. But in our lives, we do not have that power, nor is it part of your ordinary wisdom to give it to us. But you use the rhythm of love in our lives, the rhythm of holding and letting go, to draw us closer to you. When someone or something I love is taken from me, at first I feel loss, even the sense of being robbed. But Lord, grant me the grace to not simply accept the loss but to thankfully give it to you. It was yours in the first place, but you allow me the honor of freely giving it back as my gift to you. Amen.

FOR REFLECTION

1. Reflect on your own loss of a loved one. Can you trace Job's three stages in this loss?

2. Have you experienced in your life that "one never really loses what one gives to God"?

3. How have you experienced that persons, like things, attain their noblest purpose when you give them away?

CHAPTER 14

Risk and Rescue

Growing up on a ranch was an experience of force-fed maturity. When my three older brothers and I each reached the age of eight, our mother taught us to drive both car and pickup. Not on the highway, of course, but around the eight-thousand-acre ranch, where we could run errands and haul feed. I was handling a full-sized John Deere tractor at the age of nine. There was, no doubt, risk involved in this policy, but the only casualty that ever occurred was my brother Bruce's scream when he saw our apparently driverless 1936 Buick climbing a hill. (He was reassured when he finally spied me stretching my neck over the steering wheel.)

On the ranch, learning to ride horses was just as important as learning to drive, and it was taught almost as soon as we could walk. We were all broken in on a gentle mare called Pigeon. Not a great deal of risk there, but we soloed as soon as our mother would let us.

And then there was our initiation into hunting. My brother Charlie got his first buck at age eleven. I didn't find mine until fifteen (though it was, fittingly, a fifteen pointer). Austere training and rules with guns diminished the risk, but risk there was, though nothing happened more tragic than missing a shot at a prized deer or gobbler.

This risk taking to force-fed maturity was passed on to the next generation. My oldest brother, Frank, allowed his kids more slack than I would have, but there was method to his madness. When I saw his son doing acrobatics on the lake with the family fishing boat—a lake studded with underwater stumps—I said, "Frank, aren't you afraid he's going to crash into one of those stumps and get hurt?" "Well, he might, but look at what he's learning in judgment and coordination." Bubba and boat survived.

It was not so easy with the risk he took with daughter Peg. Frank loaded a double-decked eighteen-wheeler with a hundred sheep and pointed it for the market in Fort Worth, where the best time to arrive was eight o'clock in the morning, just as the market opened. That meant hauling the load through the night. Peg was barely driving age, but Frank saw this as a great chance for her to learn to drive a big rig, so he rode shotgun and let her take the wheel. She handled the truck and the sheep with skill into the night.

But near Llano, the road snakes down into a canyon. Not in itself a problem, even for Peg, unless you have a blowout on the way down. That's what happened, and at once the huge truck began to sway and the sheep were thrown to one side. In seconds, the truck, still hurtling down the canyon, capsized. Sheep were scattered over the road and the cab was inverted. Peg and Frank found themselves upside down with the roof beginning to cave in on them. Frank reached for Peg and held her tightly against the inverted seat as the windshield collapsed and the highway pavement rushed at them. Frank held Peg aloft by sheer willpower to keep her from being crushed by the pavement. It was a long time before the crippled rig lost its momentum down the hill and ground to a halt. Frank was exhausted by the ordeal, having shown the kind of superhuman strength in his arms that only a parent's love could exert in a mortal crisis. The rescue was costly, but Peg emerged unhurt.

What kind of risk did God the Father take with us? He took a risk only God could take: he gave us free will.

Why did he do that? The universe he made did not demand that it be crowned with a freewheeling creature that could mess up the whole project. Let the beauty and the grandeur of the orbs and the atoms suffice to witness to the beauty and grandeur of their Author. But witness to whom? Not to God, who didn't need their testimony. But to a creature who might be awestruck, and who might wonder where the sun and the violet and the mastodon came from, and who then might be open to encountering the Source, should that Source choose to reveal itself. And, should that happen, to discover that the Source is not a blind force, not a "what," but a "Who."

It turns out that the Creator had such an encounter in mind from the beginning. He (we can use the personal pronoun now) was constructing and adorning a home, a palace, for the kings and queens of creation to live in.

That in itself was a risk, because the occupants might become so enamored of the palace, with its delights and its comforts, that they might not hear the knocking at the door. For the God who designed the palace designed its stewards in his own image and likeness, giving them understanding and free will, that they might be open to the greatest gift of all, to know and love the Creator— in short, to be friends with him. Amazing love, amazing grace. To those who first opened the door, he showed himself, but with a veiled face: the covenant God of the Old Testament, the protector God, the *Gibor,* the Hero-God who comes to their rescue when they are trapped by oppressors—or when they are trapped by their own selfish designs, called sin. The Creator's risk was great, and sure enough, man used his mind and will to self-destruct—or try to—because although the damage of sin was so great that at one point God asked himself if maybe this whole project was a mistake, the Risker was also the Rescuer. He would not have risked unless he knew that he could rescue.

The ultimate rescue happened in the most unusual way. It was not a miracle of walling up a sea so that his people might escape the sword of Pharaoh. It was the scandal of one condemned as a criminal and nailed to a Roman cross. The rescue cost the life of the Rescuer. But the verdict of the Jewish court was reversed by the higher court, the Supreme Court of God himself, who raised Jesus from the dead and proclaimed him Savior of all who would cling to him.

The Rescue and the Revelation

As Frank's exhausting rescue of Peg showed what kind of father he was, the Father's rescue of us showed us what kind of Father he is. The rescue was a revelation. The veil on the face of this mysterious Rescuer was torn away, and we saw the face of God in a human face! The face of Jesus Christ! And if love gave Frank's arms the strength to keep Peg pinned in safety as the deadly pavement rushed at her, what is to be said of the love that kept the arms of the crucified nailed to the cross, that death might not destroy us?

Risk. Rescue. Revealer.

"Revealer" invites us to explore the mystery further. The Father took a risk not only with us. He took the supreme risk when he sent his Son. We often hear it said, "God sent his Son to die for us." There is truth in that, of course, but the saying runs roughshod over key intervening steps. Is the Father an ogre who wants to kill his Son? How can God will evil, even for the good of others? Does the end justify the means?

No. It is more complex. We must do justice to Jesus' parable about the wicked tenants (Mark 12:1-12), as we have seen in a previous chapter. The owner of the vineyard sends a series of servants to collect the fruit of the harvest. The tenants abuse one emissary after the other, even killing some of them. Finally, the owner decides to send his son, saying, "They will respect my son" (12:6). Obviously, he does not intend his son to be killed. But there is a risk, given what has happened to the previous emissaries. Still, he has faith in the goodness of the tenants: this final mission, that of the owner's own son, will succeed. But the tenants, thinking that the owner has died, plan to seize the vineyard for themselves. They kill the son and throw him out of the vineyard.

The meaning of the parable is as obvious to us as it was to its listeners. The owner of the vineyard is God; the servants sent are the Old Testament prophets; the tenants are the leaders of the Jewish people; the son is Jesus. But note these words: "They will respect my son." It is the rejection by the leaders of the Jewish people and their killing of the Son that the Father then accepts as the sacrifice that will end all other sacrifices, and the Father makes the Son the cornerstone of the new people of God. He does not rescue him from the cross, as Jesus' taunters sardonically suggest. Instead, allowing them to win their pyrrhic victory, he transforms death itself into victory by raising him from the dead, thus liberating every person from the need to fear extinction or disaster beyond the grave.

So what does this rescue reveal to us about God? That God is love? Yes, and that his love is invincible. It cannot be defeated by man's anger or rejection. When man's revolt explodes God's Plan A, God uses the rubble to make his Plan B. When we smash the vase of grace, the Father picks up the pieces and makes a mosaic—if we let him.

....

Father, there are times I wish my life were a recorder that I could rewind and record over, erasing the mistakes and sins and reliving my past the way it should have been. Why do you not allow us to do that? The reason must be that our present and our future are more important to you than our past. Your ever-present mercy is waiting to do a total makeover if we have the humility to let you do it. Please spare me from dwelling on the past and beating myself up for the wrongs I have done. Rather, let me rejoice in your forgiving and recreating grace. Amen.

FOR REFLECTION

1. Is there someone in your life who has taken a risk, perhaps greatly, for you?

2. Have you taken a great risk for anyone? What was the result?

3. What was the good and beautiful revelation that came out of Peg's catastrophe with the truck?

CHAPTER 15

Transformer

The seven hundred acres of fields on the ranch providing feed for cattle and horses were a challenge for plow and sower and reaper. And if one of those machines broke down during the window offered by the season, it could mean losing a crop. So when a plow broke that day, repair was urgent. Fortunately, five miles away there was one man who could fix the plow's twisted arm: Adolph Stricker. I was scarcely eight years old as I rode with the disabled part in the pickup to witness the repair. The swarthy blacksmith scrutinized the misshapen iron arm, then cranked up his fire and began the process of transformation. I was awed by what I saw, by what fire can do to iron. The orange rust flicked off first, and then the piece turned black. Before long the black grew red, and finally the red turned a glowing white, hardly distinguishable from the fire. At that point, Adolph was able to remove the iron, place it on his anvil, and begin to pound it into the shape he wanted.

Spiritual transformation is like that. We are twisted iron, useless and leaving untilled the world we were meant to prepare for the harvest. Then God comes along, sends the heat of his love, and we begin to change. Love purifies as it transforms. It makes us shed our rust; then it targets the darkness within us, eventually bringing us into light and making us malleable. What a wonderful parable of spiritual transformation. And is it any wonder that purgatory is depicted as fire?

If the broken plow arm could speak, it would probably scream and protest and cry out to the blacksmith, "Why are you doing this to me?" And that's how our flesh also reacts when we are hammered by trials. And even if we know in theory that God permits rather than causes evil, we can't separate our pain from our relationship with him, and so with the psalmist we cry out, "You lifted me up just to cast me down" (Psalm 102:11). Can I still think of God as our Father, even if he is only *letting* me suffer like this?

But then we open our Bible, and our eyes fall on Hebrews' reprise of Proverbs:

"My son, do not disdain the discipline of the Lord / or lose heart when reproved by him; / for whom the Lord loves, he disciplines." . . . Endure your trials as "discipline"; God treats you as sons. . . . We have had our earthly fathers to discipline us, and we respected them. Should we not [then] submit all the more to the Father of spirits and live? They disciplined us for a short time as seemed right to them, but he does so for our benefit, in order that we may share his holiness. (Hebrews 12:5-6, 7, 9-10)

We learn from the word of God that the heavenly Father disciplines and that his purpose is not to make us unhappy, nor is it merely to make us holy, but to make us share his holiness. What a difference it would make for me if every time I am struck with a trial, I would realize that this is a chance for me to grow in the very holiness of God! That is certainly not my first thought when the storm breaks, but I will try to remember that other passage from James:

> Consider it all joy, my brothers, when you encounter various trials, for you know that the testing of your faith produces perseverance. And let perseverance be perfect, so that you may be perfect and complete, lacking in nothing. (James 1:2-4)

The greatest trial in my own life was my first year teaching high school. Without any practice teaching, I found myself with five daily class preparations, four for my freshman class (religion, English, Latin, and civics) and one for a junior class (world history). Straight out of college, I made every possible mistake a beginning teacher could make and lost discipline in the class—and this lasted for a whole academic year. I certainly did not "consider it all joy." It was the first time in my life that I had failed in anything that serious. The only consolation I had was the word of an older brother, who told me, "You are experiencing redemptive suffering."

In retrospect, I realize how blessed I was to be in that crucible. I learned a lot about myself and a lot about teaching. I was on the anvil for a year. The Father was allowing me to experience the heat and the hammer, that I might grow. He also knew how much I could take. I think of Paul's word to the Corinthians: "No trial has come to you but what is human. God is faithful and will not let you be tried beyond your strength; but with the trial he will also provide a way out, so that you may be able to bear it" (1 Corinthians 10:13).

Not only that, but the word of my older brother has come back to me in other times of trial. He was summarizing Paul's word to the Colossians: "Now I rejoice in my sufferings for your sake, and in my flesh I am filling up what is lacking in the afflictions of Christ on behalf of his body, which is the church" (Colossians 1:24). Of course, Christ's sufferings are more than sufficient to save a universe, because he is God. But in terms of quantity and kind, Jesus did not suffer every kind of pain. He did not, for example, suffer the pains of old age or physical disabilities or a riotous freshman classroom. That he left for me. And that gave me hope, not just that the year would end, but that my sufferings were in the end worthwhile.

....

Father, I know it is not nature but grace that enables me to see suffering as an opportunity to grow closer to your son Jesus in his passion, and so to grow in your holiness. In my ministry I have become a wounded healer, like Jesus, whose risen glory did not erase the wounds in his hands and feet but made them windows of healing for others, not least of all for the first disbeliever— his own apostle Thomas. If I have not yet reached the holiness of rejoicing in suffering, at least let me know the joy of suffering with you. Amen.

FOR REFLECTION

1. Look back on some occasion in your life when you suffered greatly. What did you learn from it? Did you find help in your faith?

2. Can you think of someone you know who suffered greatly but found in their faith the key to survival and growth?

3. St. Paul says that God makes all things work together for good for those who love him (Romans 8:28). Can you relate an incident from your life in which you found this to be true?

CHAPTER 16

Other Fathers

Even when we have had the best of fathers, they cannot provide all we need even of fathering. God brings others into our lives to complement their role. This, of course, is all the more critical for children who have had bad experiences with their fathers. Biological fathers are not the only kind of fathers. I know—I'm one of the other kind.

While many men have done some fathering to me, three stand out at crucial periods of my life. From my earliest years, I was interested in publishing a newspaper. So at the age of seven or so, I scribbled with pencil "George's Home News" and sent copies to uncles and aunts. By the time I was eleven, I was using my father's typewriter and carbon paper and putting out regular editions, beginning to incorporate news items from beyond the family.

It was at this time that my first "complementing father" came into my life. Affable, fatherly J. Marvin Hunter, the curator of Frontier Times Museum in Bandera and publisher of the monthly "Frontier Times" (printed from a press in the back of the museum), learned of my interest in publishing and offered to print my monthly "Montague Press" free of charge. It began as a small four-page leaflet, but four years later, when I was fifteen, it had grown to a tabloid with over six hundred subscribers, and it was no longer just a family paper. I did one large issue featuring the Hereford industry in Bandera County, photos and all. The experience ended only when I felt called to the Marianist order and left home for St. Louis.

What happened to my ambition to become a newspaper publisher? From delight in crafting words, I met the Word made flesh, and my ambition morphed into a desire to serve God, and my writing skills, incubated for a number of years in the order, emerged with the two dozen or more books I have since published. But Mr. Hunter was the one who saw talent and promise in me, encouraged me, and taught me all that he knew about publishing, from hand setting type to running a press to mailing each issue and soliciting ads and subscribers. The point of all this: he was a father to me, and only years later did I come to appreciate what a great father he was. God must be something like that. He believes in us before we believe in him. He wants us to be all that he had in mind in creating us.

My second "complementing father" was Marianist Brother Roy Cherrier, my English and homeroom teacher in my sophomore and junior high school years at Central Catholic in San Antonio. He inspired me by his life but also by his teaching and especially his interest in the promise he saw in me. With the principal's permission, in my junior year he gave me my own private writing class, introducing me to Chesterton, Belloc, Karl Adam, T. S. Eliot, and C. S. Lewis, among others, while guiding my writing efforts. Again, because he saw promise, he gladly sacrificed time and effort to grow me.

My third "father" was one of our Marianist priests, Charles Blasen. As I mentioned earlier, my first year teaching high school was a disaster. At the end of the year, I found myself collapsed in a lawn chair, emotionally exhausted and wondering what the future held for me. Would they send me back to the same school? (God forbid!) That was not likely, for I felt sure the principal would ask my provincial to transfer me. But then, who would want me, and where? Was I really cut out for teaching? All kinds of scenarios ran through my mind.

Later that summer, I learned that I would be transferred to another Marianist high school in St. Louis, where Fr. Blasen, whom I had known as my philosophy teacher in college, was principal. He welcomed me warmly, and the day before I went into the classroom, he sat me down and said, "George, I want you to know I *asked* the provincial for you to be sent to this school. I know you have what it takes to be a good teacher. And there's no reason you can't start being that good teacher tomorrow morning." Here was someone who believed in me when I had plenty of reasons not to believe in myself. But with that encouragement, I went confidently into the classroom the next morning. I was amazed at the change. When the chief of the accrediting team visited our school that year, Fr. Blasen suggested he visit my classroom. When he returned, he said he had just seen outstanding teaching and that Fr. Blasen should not worry about getting the school accredited.

Is it likely this would have happened if it were not for that morning when Fr. Blasen told me he believed in me? He was indeed father to me. He taught me something about God the Father. The Father believes in us when we don't even believe in ourselves. And he sends us earthly fathers to teach us what fathering really is.

There are many others, mainly my Marianist brothers in my early religious life, to whom I should also write a tribute, but that would take another book.

Fatherly Gifts among Many

What have my experiences of other fathers taught me? First, that no human father can adequately image our heavenly Father. And if no sum of them can either, it is nevertheless true that the spread of fatherly gifts among so many teaches us the richness of God's fatherhood, for he is the source of them all. Second, deficiencies in our biological father need not prevent us from experiencing the kind of fatherhood that will enable us to make the transfer to God. I think of many young men and women I have known who, losing their biological father at a young age, found father figures in other men—in a coach, a teacher, an uncle, a priest, or perhaps a grandfather. Those who have experienced an abusive or alcoholic father have not been deprived of the father experience and thus have not been deprived of making a healthy transfer to the heavenly Father—if they were blessed with meeting other men who showed them what authentic fathering is.

I am assuming that while the father bond is most crucial for the son, it is also important for the daughter, because if the bond is strong, she will generally find herself attracted to men like her father. And the transfer to the heavenly Father is just as important for daughters as it is for sons.

And what about adoptive fathers? When an adopted child, boy or girl, takes on the name of the adopting parent, assuming the parent is strong and loving, the biological descent so recedes to the background as to become almost irrelevant. My mother's brother, taken from an orphanage, grew up with a strong bond with both his parents (my grandparents) and himself became father of a close-knit family, with his first son becoming a priest.

Finally, what does it mean to me to be "father"? Most people call me that, although I have no biological children. The title is a metaphor, transferred from biological fatherhood, because I am supposed to be a life-giver through word and sacrament and the Holy Spirit—and by the kind of generous care I have for the family of God. I think it is fair to say that I experience every day the joy and the pain of fathering, much the way biological or adoptive fathers do for their children. I do not have the intensity of responsibility that natural fathers have with their limited number of children, but no natural father is given to share the spiritual depth of relationship that a priest has with those who confide in him, especially in the confessional.

As I write this sentence, I have just come from praying with a twenty-six-year-old whom we will call Victor, whose father told him he was a mistake and then abandoned the family, leaving them with no clue even to this day of his whereabouts. What a joy for me to begin the healing process for Victor. Jesus is the doctor, but he lets me be the father.

And shortly after writing this, I received a humbling testimony from a young woman in our parish who rose from the ashes of an excruciating life, thanks in part to the ministry of the four priests (including me) who serve there:

I am truly grateful to God and you all for giving me the greatest gift called love. That love has not only touched me in such a powerfully healing and spiritual way, but it has also helped me understand, see, and feel what an awesome, loving, trusting, and merciful Father God is. My father did the best he knew how in raising me, and through Jesus, I was able not only to forgive him but also to stop blaming him for the past. I was also able to accept and love him right where he's at now, and let go of the dream that he will never be the father I have wanted and needed him to be. I thank God so much for giving me spiritual fathers who could be the father that I needed and give me what my father didn't know how to give me.

But I must never forget that before being father, I am first of all brother to everyone, and that instead of the priesthood putting me above everyone, it is a call to be servant of all. Priests are not everywhere called "Father." In the Britain of Elizabethan days, priests were called "Mister," and even today in France, they are often called "Monsieur." It doesn't matter. Priests may specialize in fathering, but they do not have a corner on the market. Spiritual fathering is open to everybody.

....

Lord, let me take some time right now to recall those who have been father to me. Whether they are still alive or have gone to your eternal embrace, I bless and thank you for them, for they were your gift to me. Without saying so, they told me something of who you are, and they helped me become a better child of yours. Bless them and let them feel the powerful tenderness of your love. And when on my journey I meet one of your children hurting from their father wound, let me do for them what you have done for me. Amen.

FOR REFLECTION

1. Think of men who have been "fathers" to you. Spend some time in prayer thanking God for each one. Then ask God to bless them.

2. How have these experiences of "father" complemented the experience of your own father?

3. What kinds of qualities would you expect to find in a spiritual father? How would these qualities reflect those of God the Father?

CHAPTER 17

Jesus, Icon of the Father

"No one has ever seen God. The only Son, who is God, ever in the Father's embrace, has revealed him" (John 1:18, my translation). In chapter 12, we asked what we could learn about Jesus resting on the Father's breast by contemplating him as a child resting on the breast of Mary. But now we need to explore how this resting on the Father's breast played out in Jesus' public life. In answer to Philip's request, "Show us the Father," Jesus said, "Philip, whoever sees me sees the Father" (John 14:8-9, my translation). What was it that Philip didn't realize in the three years he had spent with Jesus? Or to put it another way, how can we see the Father revealed in those three years, which climaxed with the death and resurrection of Jesus and the sending of the Holy Spirit?

The Gospels multiply scenes from the life of this carpenter of Nazareth, and from them we can begin to sense what is causing the eternal Son to act as the time-bound Son. When he came to earth, he never left the eternal embrace. He showed what it meant humanly and, more important, what it meant for us who would be called to join him in that embrace.

So Jesus, what was your passion, your dream, your holy addiction as you rose from the Jordan waters and confronted the world of man? What was going on in your mind and heart as your feet walked on the sands that we call the "Holy Land" because you walked upon them? The Gospels tell us that the first word on your lips was "the kingdom." It was the meeting point of your dream, which was the Father's dream, and the hollow dream of your people. Two very different dreams, but a starting point nonetheless. About the time you were born, a Jew from Galilee had rallied four hundred armed men to bring about "the kingdom of God." The project failed, but it showed that there was hope, there was expectation, there was readiness for a leader. So at least you had an audience. Your forerunner John had a different idea of your coming. You would be the fiery judge, the harvest that would thresh wheat from flame-destined chaff.

But your actions trumped them all. You began to heal, to comfort, to forgive and teach forgiveness, to reach out to those crushed under the weight of rejection. You confronted the mighty and raised the lowly. You said that the last would be first and the first last, that the least is really the greatest, that the kingdom is made not by the fist of the mighty but by the heart and hand of the servant. And the followers you gathered did not even carry a walking stick (Mathew 10:10). The powerful were at first dismayed, then threatened, and then fired up to plot your destruction. Even John the Baptist had his doubts and sent his disciples to ask whether you were really the mighty one he had foretold. Should they look for someone else? (11:3). Your reply was that you had come not to judge but to save from judgment. And you pointed to the army of the healed who would become the healers of the wounded world. That is how the kingdom would come.

What was happening was that the interpersonal union of the eternal embrace—Father, Son, and Holy Spirit, the perfect pattern of union in love—was in Jesus confronting a world so unfamiliar with that vision that its response could only be either radical resistance or radical conversion. Like the collision of a cold front with a warm front, the resulting storm would take the life of Jesus and the martyrs after him, and mark all his followers with the cross.

But just as the storm releases the refreshing rain, new life springs up where death had seemed to triumph. Jesus leaves the tomb forever, the martyrs' blood falls to the ground as seed preparing a harvest of Christians, and those spared martyrdom are empowered to be heroes of daily life. The paschal mystery is the human language of the divine Three. In a world sullied by hatred, bloodshed, selfishness, and lust, the Three cannot speak the language of glory without first speaking the language of the cross, entering into the world's misery and saving it from within. No *deus ex machina*, a Greek god rescuing from without, but *deus ex cruce*, the God who knows human suffering from within because he died crucified. Love faithful unto death reveals the Father's face and the Father's heart, for "God so loved the world that he gave his only Son, so that everyone who believes in him might not perish but might have eternal life" (John 3:16).

So if we want to see the Father, if we want to feel his embrace, we need to follow the route by which he came to save us: the gift of Jesus, "the Way," and the Holy Spirit, who empowers us with the cry "*Abba*." There is no authentic union with the Father that is not created by these two. For the love in which we share is the inter-Trinitarian love, not some other love, not even the love merely of a creator God, but the one who has revealed to us the secret of his own inner life and invited us to share it.

And that love, that life, is meant for everyone, as we shall see in the next chapter. It is the key to bringing about the kingdom for which Jesus laid down his life and for which he told us to pray, to make earth a mirror of heaven.

....

Lord Jesus, do not let me be like Philip, missing the revelation of the mystery right in front of me. You are the earthly revelation of the Father's face. Empower me with your Holy Spirit, that I may see the Father's face in yours. Amen.

FOR REFLECTION

1. Think of one way the life of Jesus reveals the inner life of the Trinity.

2. Why is it necessary for authentic followers of Jesus to be marked with the cross? How has this played out in your life?

3. Jesus has commissioned us to continue his work of bringing about the kingdom. How do we do it?

Chapter 18

Brothers and Sisters

How many Indians can ride in a Jeep?" I asked myself after counting twenty-four of them in and on a Jeep for the hour-long ride from the remote village of Sokho in northern India to the nearest bus stop. The answer, I concluded, was "one more." I had joined the rolling beehive at about number seventeen and spent the hour straddling the one-inch wide sideboard with my tailbone, half of me outside the jeep and clinging to the roof. We can't hold one more, I thought every time we stopped for another, only to be proved wrong. When we passed the two-dozen mark, I made sure my math was right. With me, it was twenty-five.

The ride proved one thing to me: we humans are not angels, any multitude of whom can dance together on the head of a pin. We are space-displacing people, and no matter how much we try to squeeze together, we need our own space. Indians, no matter how many, are not angels, and neither am I.

That is true of all things material. But in the realm of the spiritual, is there a limit to how many can come together and even become one? And is this true of our experience of the Father? On earth, intimacy means a deep union of you and me, and it is threatened by numbers. If I invite you to a restaurant for lunch with the hope of discussing some serious issue, I look for a spot as distant from the crowd as possible. How, then, can I have the most intimate union with the Father and yet share that with a universe of others?

So taken was I with the image of Colonel Stirm and his daughter in that breathtaking reunion, and so taken was I with the effects of a personal encounter with the Father, that I entitled this book "Living in the Father's Embrace." My editor thought that a better title would be "Living in *Our* Father's Embrace," since Catholics, and other Christians as well, would hear the echo of the "Our Father" when they looked at the title. I pondered her suggestion a long time and asked some friends which title seemed the better. But then I reread the first seventeen chapters and saw that all of them were more concerned with the vertical personal relationship with the Father than with the horizontal bond with others.

Why this emphasis? Certainly I did not mean that the relationship with the Father should be individualistic or exclusive. Quite the contrary. Often what keeps us from truly relating to each other as brothers and sisters is that we do not have a personal understanding, much less an encounter, with God as our *Abba*, Father. Sometimes, as in the restaurant, it is necessary to get away from the crowd to address deeply personal issues—like healing the father wound—*that are keeping the child of God from a healthy relationship with the Father's other children and with the rest of the world.* The core issue addressed in this book is the person's image of and relationship with the Person of God the Father. When I don't understand who God is and how I'm meant to relate to him, I will fall short in my relations with others. Accordingly, the first seventeen chapters of this book have addressed intensely those personal issues like the relationship with our earthly fathers.

But once healed and feeling the Father's embrace, I will want to burst out of my booth and share my joy with everyone else in the restaurant. They are my brothers and sisters!

Blessing, Not Competition

What a difference that makes! I discovered this reality quite late in life, when the Father, Jesus, and the Holy Spirit gave me the grace of "traffic conversion." That's the name I give to the experience of seeing other drivers not as my competitors but as my brothers and sisters. Of course, my siblings' driving can be worse than strangers' driving, but that does not make them any less my brothers and sisters. And yes, it makes a big difference whether I see them as my kin; in fact, as my brothers and sisters, for indeed such they are in Christ. They share—or are meant to share—the same intimacy with the Father to which I am called. And if for some reason—distraction, impatience, impulsiveness, or bullying—they have not tasted the Father's love, it is there, waiting for them. And they need blessing rather than competition or, worse yet, road rage.

When I was a teenager and riding with some family member on the endless highways in west Texas, it was taken for granted that one driver passing another (a rather rare event) would wave, as if to say, "Oh, I'm so glad to see another human being in this barren land." But in our crowded cities today, we are grateful to find an open road, and in congestion the exchange of hand signals, when it happens, usually means anything but "I'm glad to see you."

One day I had pulled out of a Walmart parking lot onto the access road of I-410 and found myself behind a truck whose driver must have been trained by a sloth. Intending to pass him, I checked to see if the adjacent lane was clear. It was, save for a car so far behind me that it posed no problem. So I pulled into the next lane, and by the time I was moving beside the truck, that distant car loomed at my rear, telling me that its driver was speeding and was vexed even at my proper speed. As soon as I cleared the truck, he swerved into the lane in front of the truck. As he swept past, he flashed me with the kind of finger greeting we all recognize. I thought to raise my hand in blessing but then decided not to, lest he think I was responding in kind. But a blessing was in my heart. I don't always respond that way, but I am learning to, as I try to remember, "That's my brother," or "That's my sister."

That's not make-believe—if God is our Father.

And that's what Jesus would say if he were riding with me.

....

Father, thank you for teaching me that the closer I get to you, the closer I get to others, seeing your reflection in them and your promise. Do not let me be turned off by their appearance or their manners. May I be like Jesus with everyone I encounter. Let them see in me a reflection of the great love that in Jesus you showed for the least and most needy. Teach me to embrace them as you have embraced me. Amen.

FOR REFLECTION

1. How often do I consciously see another person as a child of God?

2. What might be preventing me from seeing others not as competitors but as "kin"? What type of healing might I need to relate to others in a more loving way?

3. Jesus was conscious of the Father's love and shared it in everything he did. How do I experience the Father's love in the various activities of my life, like traffic?

CHAPTER 19

The Father Embraces His Family

The triangle and the shamrock: two images by which the religious sisters in grade school tried to get the mystery of the Trinity into my head. In the second-grade band, I played the triangle, trying my best to hit it on the right beat. The shamrock was, of course, the favorite image used by the Irish nuns. Both were sufficient for me at that age to get an idea of what was, after all, a mystery even to grown-ups.

But as I grew into adulthood, I saw how material things, no matter how beautiful in tone or texture or taste, fell terribly short of what I was learning about Father, Son, and Holy Spirit. They were Persons, and so I looked to human persons for a better door to the mystery. More important, I began to see in human relationships a closer key to what theology would call the "substantial relations" in the Holy Trinity. The name of the key: marriage and the family. The love of a man and woman bears fruit in their offspring. And where there is perfect love, there is unity.

Of course, the differences between the family and the Holy Trinity are greater than the likenesses. God the Father generates the Word as his image, and the Holy Spirit proceeds from their mutual embrace by way of the sigh of love. They are distinct Persons, though one in nature.

There is the mystery: how can three distinct persons be one? It would be helpful to reflect that at least in our human experience, we know that all love drives the lover and the beloved toward unity. The heart would like to consume and be consumed by the other. In marriage the two become one flesh, while preserving their distinction. In God the difference of Persons remains, but their unity is not only a unity of love but a unity of being. And this unity blossoms in the Holy Spirit, fruit of their mutual love.

Now what does this mean practically for us? How does love move from unity to the transcendence of self and then to fruitfulness? In marriage, the impulse to unity begins when two people fall in love; then they wish to seal their love in a lifelong commitment. The impulse to unity does not end there. It is rather the beginning of a lifelong journey of discovery of one another, and discovery of self in the process. The union grows deeper as the rust of egoism is burned away and results not in a greater possession of one another but in an opening out to transcending themselves. As the French writer Antoine de Saint-Exupéry put it, "Love does not consist in gazing at each other but in looking outward together in the same direction."

One of the chief ways in which this transcending of self happens is in the begetting and rearing of children. The couple's love grows and is completed by their mutual investment in the life project of new human beings. And this in turn leads the couple to work toward an environment that fosters life. In other words, the family begins to fulfill its role as the basic unit of society, working to make that society a worthy home for their family and the whole family of God.

Most couples do this without reflecting on their noble role. Fewer realize that what they are doing is living out the life of the Trinity in human terms. But that is what they are doing. Unfortunately, in today's world of individualism, those who try to live the ideal find themselves in a struggle with a culture that increasingly sees marriage only in terms of self-satisfying love, a deception like orchard trees with blooms that never bear fruit.

If marriage begins with the Trinity, that is where it will end. Jesus says that in heaven, there is no marriage. Couples who have lived their lives in a happy union may feel disappointed when they hear that. What happens to all the joy we have felt together? What happens if I have lost my spouse here? Will I have no joy at meeting him or her again?

No. Nothing will be lost, for even married joy here, no matter how ecstatic, is limited. It longs for and points to an ever-greater fulfillment. And that's because there *is* marriage in heaven. It is the marriage of the Lamb with his bride, the Church in glory. And there, every holy union on earth finds its ultimate destiny at last achieved. For the couple is wed now, not till death do them part, but for all eternity, for they have found the fount of all love, the source from which their married love has flowed, the spousal love of Christ for his Church, of which their married love was the icon. Yes, even marriages that were rocky, even marriages that failed on earth, even marriages that for whatever reason led to second marriages, these will all dissolve like raindrops in the infinite ocean of God's love.

Isaac sent his son Jacob in search of a bride (Genesis 28:1-5). The Father sent his Son in search of a bride too. He found her squalid but beautiful beneath the filth. He washed her with his own blood, claimed her as his own, and set on her finger a diamond of promise, sparkling already with the glory of heaven, where the wedding will be consummated. "Come here," says the angel in the Apocalypse. "I will show you the bride, the wife of the Lamb" (Revelation 21:9). From a high mountain, John sees the bride: it is the holy city, the new Jerusalem (21:10). The bride is all the redeemed. As Jesus' spouse in glory, they join him in the great wedding feast.

But that is not all. Jesus has a wedding gift for his bride: it is the Father's embrace. For Jesus lives in that embrace, and his ultimate gift to his bride is to bring her with him to the Father's breast, that Father "from whom every family in heaven and on earth is named" (Ephesians 3: 15).

....

Married or not, I learn from marriage something about your inner life, my God. You are indeed not a solitary, distant force, but three dynamic Persons so united as to be one not merely in love but in your very being. If this mystery defies my ability to understand, it nevertheless inspires me to live beyond the limits of what my mind and heart can grasp. "'What eye has not seen, and ear has not heard, / and what has not entered the human heart, / what God has prepared for those who love him,' this God has revealed to us through the Spirit" (1 Corinthians 2:9-10). I live now in anticipation of the great wedding feast, where with all my dear ones, I will enjoy with you, Lord Jesus, the Father's eternal embrace. May it be so. Amen.

FOR REFLECTION

1. In what ways is marriage an image of the Trinity? In what ways is it not?

2. "All love tends both to unity and to fruitfulness." Why do you think this is the case? When have you seen this in your life?

3. How is it possible for married love to be fulfilled in heaven by going beyond itself?

CHAPTER 20

Jesus Prays to His Father for Us

The Old Testament Jews had a keen sense that sin must be atoned for. Their failings against God's covenant must be made up for, covered, wiped away, deleted. They did this mainly by offering sacrifices of grain, incense, or animals. In most cases, it was individual Jews who brought their offering to the priest. But on one day of the year, the feast of the Atonement, Jews flocked together as a people for a liturgy they believed would wipe away the sins of the last year for all the people.

Here's how it happened. The high priest would take a bowl of blood from a sacrificed animal and enter the Holy of Holies where the ark of the covenant was kept behind a veil. None but the high priest was allowed to do this, and only once a year. He would then dip his finger into the blood and use it to cleanse the propitiatory, the front part of the ark. This symbolized his cleansing the site of God's presence from the sins of the people that had contaminated it during the past year. When finished, he would come out and bless the people with prayer.

Some scholars see this scene as background for what has been called "Jesus' priestly prayer" in chapter 17 of John's Gospel. Jesus has taken the blood of his own sacrifice on the cross and "passed through the veil" into the presence of the Father and cleansed his people of their sins, reconciling them with God once and for all. Then, as if already in heaven, he asks the Father's blessing on the people reconciled by his blood. A blessing is a special prayer addressed to God.

But the prayer is more than the unique blessing made possible by Jesus' sacrifice. It is also his personal farewell blessing, a blessing that, like many blessings, includes intercession for those he is leaving. And finally, it echoes the prayer that Jesus taught his disciples.

Earlier, in chapter 3, we saw the disciples "eavesdropping" on Jesus' prayer. When asked to teach them to pray, Jesus said, "When *you* pray, say . . . " (Luke 11:2, emphasis mine). But in Jesus' priestly prayer, we hear his own version of this prayer when he himself addresses the Father. There are many similarities with the Our Father. It is not surprising that just as Jesus taught his disciples to begin with the word "Father," he would also begin here with the same sacred yet affectionate address: "Father," *Abba!* (John 17:1). At this climactic moment in Jesus' life, on the eve of his total self-gift on the cross, we hear the earthly expression of the eternal relationship of the second Person of the Trinity to the first—one earthly sound, one earthly word that contains the entire self-revelation of God In the synoptic Gospels, we hear it on the lips of Jesus struggling with the Father in the garden prior to his passion. Here we hear it as the "liftoff" into glory. How can this be, since Jesus faces the most brutal suffering the world has ever known? It is not simply that Jesus sees the light of his resurrection already stealing beneath the dark door of the cross. Rather, it is the glory of the act of Love itself, Jesus' gift of himself to the Father, for your sake and mine.

It is the hour when the Father will glorify Jesus as Jesus glorifies the Father. Thus, Jesus begins, "Father, the hour has come. Give glory to your son, so that your son may glorify you, just as you gave him authority over all people, so that he may give eternal life to all you gave him" (John 17:1-2). This is Jesus' version of "Hallowed be thy name," which means, "Show the glory of your name." Jesus has never left the Father's embrace, so the gift of himself on the cross is also the Father's gift: the cross reveals the mutual love of Father and Son. "I glorified you on earth by accomplishing the work that you gave me to do. Now glorify me, Father, with you, with the glory that I had with you before the world began" (17:4-5). It was as if Jesus were saying, "Let the cross reveal on earth the glory of our eternal embrace." "The Father loves his Son" (5:20) and "The world must know that I love the Father" (14:31).

The Beauty of Sacrificial Love

It is easy to see how the cross would be the highest expression of Jesus' love for the Father. And it is easy to see how the cross would express the Father's love for the world: "God so loved the world that he gave his only Son" (John 3:16). But how does the cross reveal the Father's love for the Son, whom he sent on such a mortal mission? It can only be because Father and Son are one in their desire to manifest to the world the horror of sin and the beauty of sacrificial love. Here is where every soldier dying on a battlefield can find meaning for his life, where every mother walking a crying baby at two in the morning finds meaning for her life, where every sacrifice for another shows the real meaning of love.

In the Our Father, we pray, "Thy kingdom come." The Jesus of John's Gospel speaks of the kingdom on only two occasions: first, with Nicodemus, who must be born of water and the Spirit to enter "the kingdom of God" (3:3, 5), and second, with Pilate, who must learn that Jesus' kingdom is not of this world (18:36). We would expect Jesus to say something about the kingdom in this prayer, but for the Jesus of John's Gospel, the kingdom is love, and it is experienced where there is mutual love and where there is unity in mutual love. Thus, Jesus here prays for unity among all his disciples. Although he came to save the world that God loves (3:16), it is not for the world that he prays but for the disciples of all ages, because it is only in the intimacy of a united community that the world will really experience heaven on earth, the Father's embrace. And such a community will tell the world that Jesus is the way to its salvation.

"I pray . . . that they may all be one, as you, Father, are in me and I in you, that they also may be in us, that the world may believe that you sent me . . . , that the love with which you loved me may be in them and I in them" (John 17:20-21, 26). There is no clearer passage of Scripture than this to confirm what this book has been about. Our call, our destiny, is to be caught up in the mutual love of Father and Son and to know the overwhelming joy of their embrace. That love is essentially the Holy Spirit, and it is the Spirit that enables us to receive and to give love that goes beyond our capacities, to live heroically with him who lived and died heroically for us, the Father's beloved Son.

Unity among the disciples—and that means unity among us—is not the only way to evangelize, of course, but it is an important condition: "That the world may believe that you sent me." The reason is that sharing in the intimate life of the Trinity is the ultimate goal of all evangelization, whether it be direct by proclamation, or by way of witness, or through service. And if people can see the unity of love in the Trinity reflected in the unity of love in the Christian community, the attraction will be virtually irresistible. "See how they love one another," the pagans said of the first Christians. And that led scores of them to embrace the faith and, in so doing, to enter the Father's embrace. It was not only the miracle of the resurrection that won the pagan world to embrace the cross; it was also the miracle of love and unity they saw before their very eyes.

....

Father, you have called us to live on earth as we will live in heaven—enjoying with Jesus your embrace. And that challenges us to grow into and preserve the "unity of the spirit through the bond of peace" (Ephesians 4:3) so that we may reflect to the world your own mysterious unity, three Persons in one God. But just as your own goodness overflows, so must the goodness you have given us. You do not want us to be a ghetto. If your gospel fashions losers and loners into lovers, the school you have given us in which we learn to love is the Christian community. If we cannot love one another, how will we ever learn to love our enemies? But with your Holy Spirit, we can love beyond the limits of the human heart. We can love as Jesus loves. Teach us, Lord, to love. Amen.

FOR REFLECTION

1. How does self-sacrifice show the real meaning of love? Where do you see this in your own life?

2. The unity that Jesus prays for is the unity that he wishes for your family, for every nation, and for every group linked together by natural or fashioned bonds. Do you enter into Jesus' prayer for unity for your family, for all Christians, and for the world, that it will come to know the God who is the source of all unity?

3. What else might you do to strengthen bonds in these groups?

About the Author

 Fr. George Montague, a Marianist priest, was born and grew up on a Texas ranch, from which he often makes parables of his experiences. Ordained a priest in 1958, he received his doctorate in biblical studies from the University of Fribourg in Switzerland in 1960. He has served his community in various ministries: as professor of Scripture at St. Mary's University for thirty-one years, as seminary rector in St. Louis and Toronto, and as director of Indian Marianist novices in Kathmandu, Nepal. Former president of the Catholic Biblical Association of America and editor of the *Catholic Biblical Quarterly*, he is the author of two dozen books on Scripture and spirituality. He is also cofounder of a new religious community of priests and brothers, the Brothers of the Beloved Disciple.

the**WORD**
among us ®
The *Spirit* of Catholic Living

T his book was published by The Word Among Us. Since 1981, The
Word Among Us has been answering the call of the Second Vatican Council
to help Catholic laypeople encounter Christ in the Scriptures.

The name of our company comes from the prologue to the Gospel of
John and reflects the vision and purpose of all of our publications: to be an
instrument of the Spirit, whose desire is to manifest Jesus' presence in and
to the children of God. In this way, we hope to contribute to the Church's
ongoing mission of proclaiming the gospel to the world so that all people
would know the love and mercy of our Lord and grow ever more deeply
in love with him.

Our monthly devotional magazine, *The Word Among Us*, features medi-
tations on the daily and Sunday Mass readings, and currently reaches more
than one million Catholics in North America and another half million
Catholics in one hundred countries around the world. Our book division,
The Word Among Us Press, publishes numerous books, Bible studies, and
pamphlets that help Catholics grow in their faith.

To learn more about who we are and what we publish, log on to our
website at www.wau.org. There you will find a variety of Catholic resources
that will help you grow in your faith.

Embrace His Word, Listen to God . . .

www.wau.org